Welcome to
the fucking world
of Swearing...

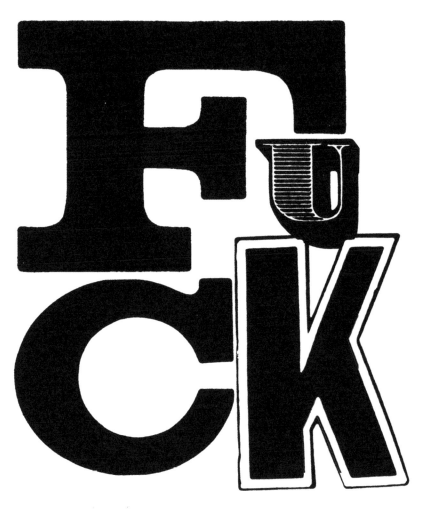

THE F!$*@ING HISTORY OF SWEARING

CONTENT

PROLOGUE

Swearing is and always has been regarded as undereducated, obscene, rude and profane in society. It has been censored, forbidden and the institutions of power continue to ban it from society and all media. Due to censorship there are groups of people who fight against swearing, certain religions who think the devil is the father of "fuck" and whole hordes of mothers who don't want their kids to say words like shit, piss fuck or cunt.For some these words are dirty and bad and you shouldn't say them. Ever. Yet despite your mum's best efforts,cussing is mainstream.

It's even more than that, it's an integrated part of our culture. We have used profane language since the beginning of time, and when I say "we", I mean people in all countries, all over the world, in every language, dialect, slang or accent studied, living or dead, in big cities to small tribes in the middle of nowhere, they all turn out to have their own "forbidden speech". Yet, why is there this goddamned societal discomfort when a casual "fuck yeah" accompanied with a high five can make you feel so awesome?

Shit! Fuck! Damn! Piss off! The number of times we swear

is huge. It happens almost automatically and you would have to almost force yourself if you'd want to stop using them. We don't plan to use them, you wouldn't think twice about shouting the word "fuck" if you were to hurt yourself. It happens automatically and that's the interesting point. So is swearing an instinct then? Where did it actually come from and when the fuck did it become such a bad thing? What's the fucking history of swearing? What is the roof of people's discomfort with swearing and what exactly is objectionable about profanity? Where do we draw the line?

Or do we even need to draw a line at all? Where does the hidden power of these words even come from? Why does it make you feel so great?
Could we use the power of these words and phrases wisely as a tool in our daily life and appreciate the fact that we have them and their emotional effect on us?
Having spent some time on searching and looking for the answers to these questions I encountered a treasure trove of interesting information on this beautifully offensive topic.
What you have before you is my research; filtered, condensed and bundled together,

giving an overview of the highly expletive world of swearing. The swearing atlas; a guide to the world of profanity. So lean back, grab a cup of some fucking hot or cold beverage, fasten your seat belt and enjoy the swearing atlas to the full. Bon fucking voyage!

IN THE BEGINNING...

...God created the heavens and the
earth. Now the earth was formless
and empty, darkness was over
surface of the deep, and the Spirit
of God was hovering over the waters.

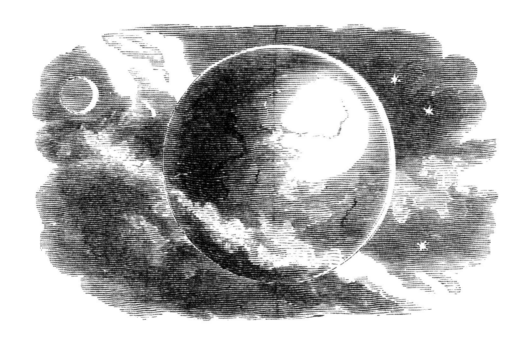

(this was the very first part of the Holy Bible,
the start of everything. The Bible also says t hat
God knows everything and.isn't such a big fan of
swearing...)

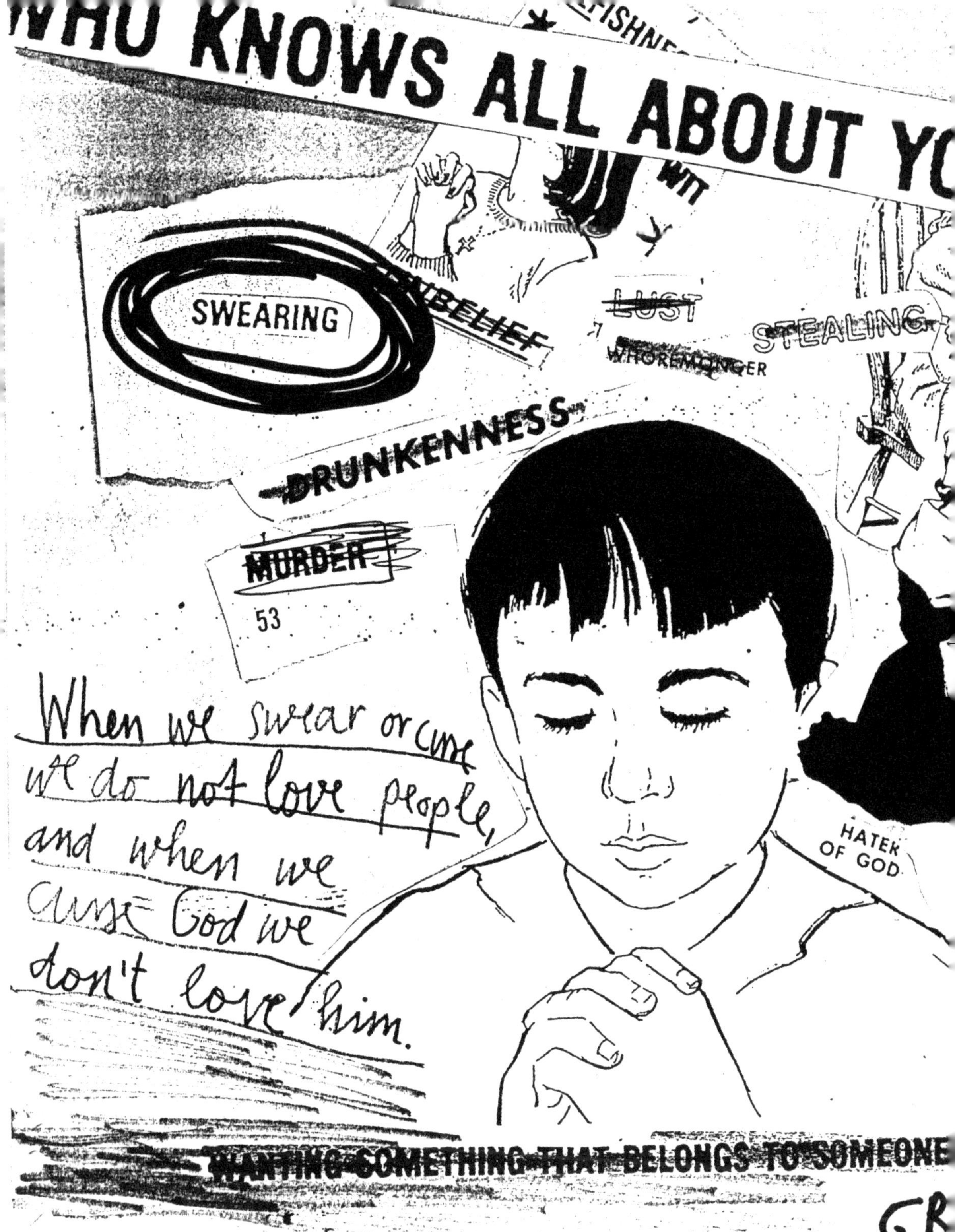

SWEARING

DISBELIEF

LUST

STEALING

WHOREMONGER

DRUNKENNESS

MURDER

53

When we swear or curse
we do not love people,
and when we
curse God we
don't love him.

HATER
OF GOD

WANTING SOMETHING THAT BELONGS TO SOMEONE

The Holy Bible tells us that it's definitely a sin to curse

GR
LOVE

R SINS?

GAY

GOD.

FROM THE BIBLICAL DEFINITION OF SIN, OUR OVERVIEW OF CURSING & SWEARING AND SCRIPTURE'S MANY EXPRESSIONS ON THE USE OF OUR TONGUE IT'S WITHOUT QUESTION A SIN TO CURSE.

CURSING IS CONTRARY TO RESTING ON GOD'S PROMISES, FOR IT IS A FAILURE TO FOLLOW THE LORDS TEST COMMANDMENTS - TO OD AND TO LOVE PEOPLE.

(matthew 22:37-4)

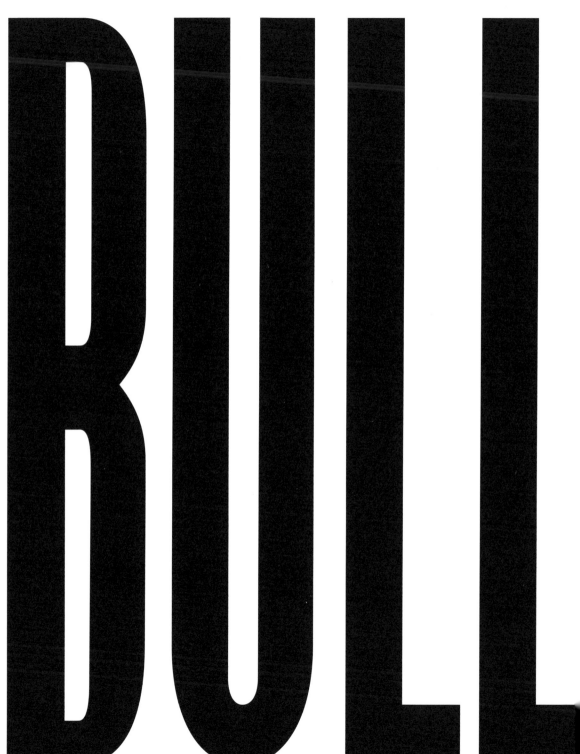

BULL

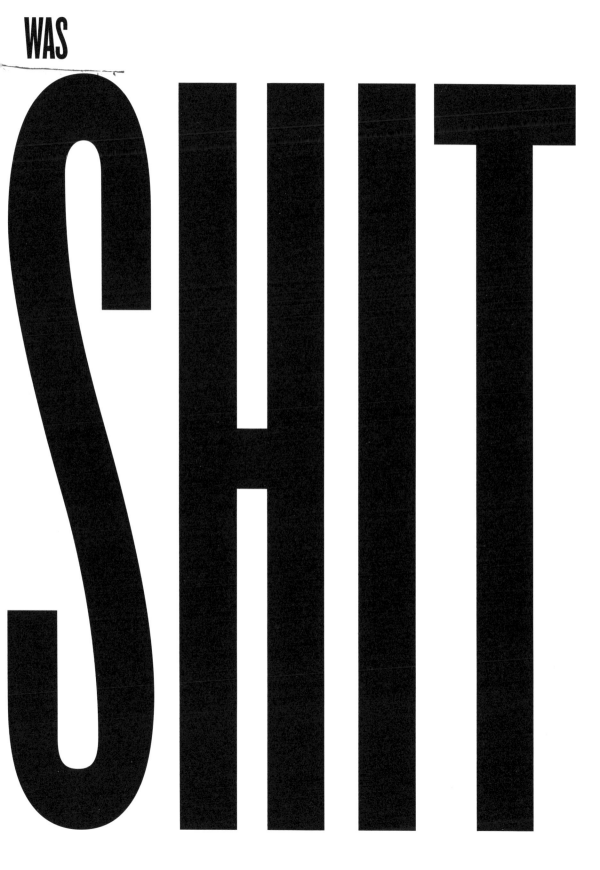

BECAUSE THAT BOY

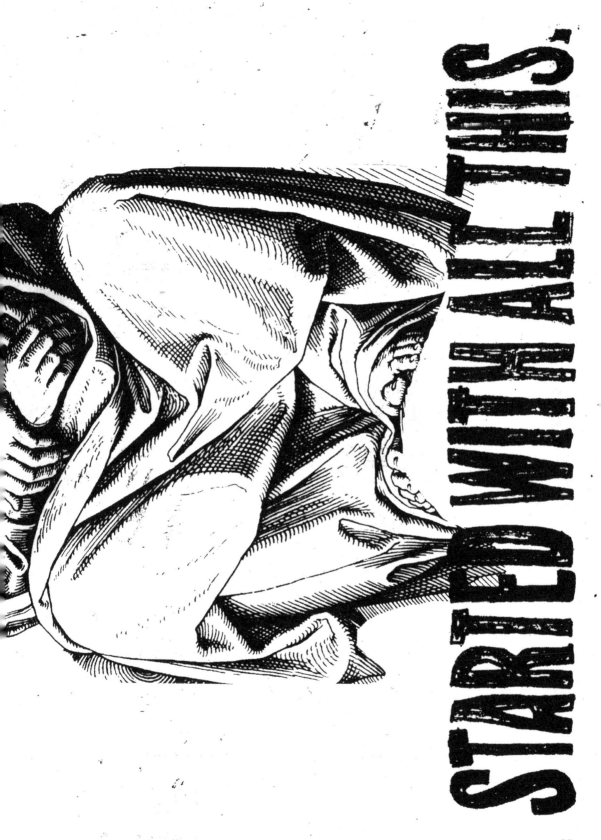

STARTED WITH ALL THIS,'

ACTUALLY WHAT HAPPENED IS, THAT GOD TOLD THE SNAKE TO FUCK OFF ON PAGE THREE IN THE OLD TESTAMENT:

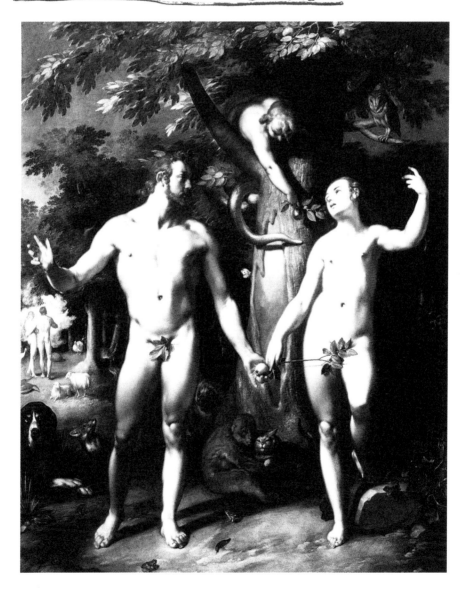

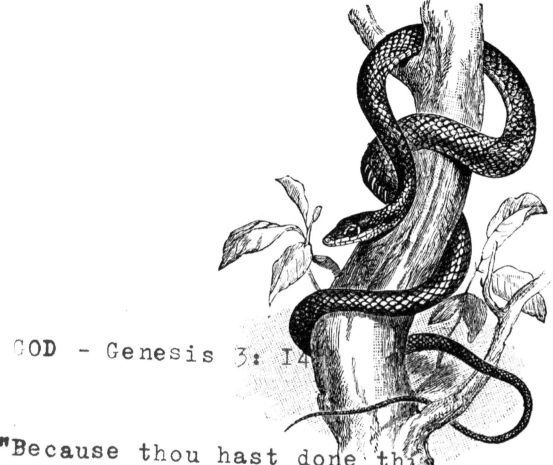

GOD - Genesis 3: 14

"Because thou hast done this
thou art cursed above every
beast of the field; Upon the
belly shalt thou go, and dust
shalt thou eat all the days of
thy life."

AMEN

creepeth upon the earth after his kind: and God saw that *it was* good.

26 And God said, [t]Let us make man in our image, after our likeness: and [u]let them have dominion over the fish of the sea, and over the fowl of the air, and over the cattle, and over all the earth, and over every creeping thing that creepeth upon the earth.

27 So God created man in his *own* image, [v]in the image of God created he him; [w]male and female created he them.

28 And God blessed them, and God said unto them, [x]Be fruitful, and multiply, and replenish the earth, and subdue it: and have dominion over the fish of the sea, and over the fowl of the air, and over every living thing that [k]moveth upon the earth.

29 And God said, Behold, I have given you every herb [l]bearing seed, which *is* upon the face of all the earth, and every tree, in the which *is* the fruit of a tree yielding seed; [y]to you it shall be for meat.

30 And to [z]every beast of the earth, and to every [a]fowl of the air, and to every thing that creepeth upon the earth, wherein *there is* [m]life, I have given every green herb for meat: and it was so.

31 And [b]God saw every thing that he had made, and, behold, *it was* very good. And the evening and the morning were the sixth day.

2 THUS THE heavens and the earth were finished, and [c]all the host of them.

2 [d]And on the seventh day God ended his work which he had made; and he rested on the seventh day from all his work which he had made.

3 And God [e]blessed the seventh day, and sanctified it: because that in it he had rested from all his work which God [n]created and made.

Adam and Eve

4 [f]These *are* the generations of the heavens and of the earth when they were created, in the day that the LORD God made the earth and the heavens,

5 And every [g]plant of the field before it was in the earth, and every herb of the field before it grew: for the LORD God had not [h]caused it to rain upon the earth, and *there was* not a man [i]to till the ground.

6 But [o]there went up a mist from the earth, and watered the whole face of the ground.

7 And the LORD God formed man [p]of the [j]dust of the ground, and [k]breathed into his [l]nostrils the breath of life; and [m]man became a living soul.

8 And the LORD God planted [n]a garden [o]eastward in [p]Eden; and there he put the man whom he had formed.

9 And out of the ground made the LORD God to grow [q]every tree that is pleasant to the sight, and good for food; [r]the tree of life also in the midst of the garden, and the tree of knowledge of good and evil.

10 And a river went out of Eden to water the garden; and from thence it was parted, and became into four heads.

11 The name of the first *is* Pison: that *is* it which compasseth [s]the whole land of Havilah, where *there is* gold;

12 And the gold of that land *is* good: [t]there *is* bdellium and the onyx stone.

13 And the name of the second river *is* Gihon: the same *is* it that compasseth the whole land of [q]Ethiopia.

14 And the name of the third river *is* [u]Hiddekel: that *is* it which goeth [r]toward the east of Assyria. And the fourth river *is* Euphrates.

15 And the LORD God took [s]the man, and put him into the garden of Eden to dress it and to keep it.

16 And the LORD God commanded the man, saying, Of every tree of the garden [t]thou mayest freely eat:

17 But of the tree of the knowledge of good and evil, [v]thou shalt not eat of it: for in the day that thou eatest thereof [w]thou[u] shalt surely die.

18 And the LORD God said, It is not good that the man should be alone; [x]I will make him an help [v]meet for him.

19 [y]And out of the ground the LORD God formed every beast of the field, and every fowl of the air; and [z]brought *them* unto [w]Adam to see what he would call them: and whatsoever Adam called every living creature, that *was* the name thereof.

20 And Adam [x]gave names to all cattle, and to the fowl of the air, and to every beast of the field; but for Adam there was not found an help meet for him.

21 And the LORD God caused a [a]deep sleep to fall upon Adam, and he slept: and he took one of his ribs, and closed up the flesh instead thereof;

22 And the rib, which the LORD God had taken from man, [y]made he a woman, and [b]brought her unto the man.

23 And Adam said, This *is* now [c]bone of my bones, and flesh of my flesh: she shall be called [z]Woman, because she was [d]taken out of [a]Man.

24 [e]Therefore shall a man leave his father and his mother, and shall cleave unto his wife: and they shall be one flesh.

25 [f]And they were both naked, the man and his wife, and were not [g]ashamed.

1:26
[t]Ps. 100:3
Eccl. 7:29
Eph. 4:24
Jas. 3:9
[u]ch. 9:2
Ps. 8:6

1:27
[v]1 Cor. 11:7
[w]ch. 5:2
Mat. 19:4

1:28
[x]ch. 9:1,7
Lev. 26:9

1:29
[y]ch. 9:3
Ps. 104:14,15

1:30
[z]Ps. 145:15
[a]Job 38:41

1:31
[b]Ps. 104:24

2:1
[c]Ps. 33:6

2:2
[d]Ex. 20:11
Heb. 4:4

2:3
[e]Is. 58:13

2:4
[f]ch. 1:1

2:5
[g]ch. 1:12
[h]Job 38:26-28
[i]ch. 3:23

2:7
[j]ch. 3:19,23
Ps. 103:14
[k]Job 33:4
[l]ch. 7:22
[m]1 Cor. 15:45

2:8
[n]Is. 51:3
[o]ch. 3:24
[p]ch. 4:16

2:9
[q]Ezek. 31:8
[r]ch. 3:22
Rev. 2:7

2:11
[s]ch. 25:18

2:12
[t]Num. 11:7

2:14
[u]Dan. 10:4

2:17
[v]ch. 3:1,3,11,17
[w]ch. 3:3,19
Rom. 6:23

2:18
[x]1 Cor. 11:9
1 Tim. 2:13

2:19
[y]ch. 1:20,24
[z]Ps. 8:6

2:21
[a]1 Sam. 26:12

2:22
[b]Heb. 13:4

2:23
[c]ch. 29:14
Eph. 5:30
[d]1 Cor. 11:8

2:24
[e]Mat. 19:5
Eph. 5:31

2:25
[f]ch. 3:7,10
[g]Is. 47:3

---

[k]Heb. *creepeth*   [l]Heb. *seeding seed*
[m]Heb. *a living soul*   [n]Heb. *created to make*
[o]Or, *a mist which went up from*   [p]Heb.
dust of the ground   [q]Heb. *Cush*   [r]Or,
eastward to Assyria   [s]Or, *Adam*   [t]Heb.
eating thou shalt eat   [u]Heb. *dying thou
shalt die*   [v]Heb. *as before him*   [w]Or, *the
man*   [x]Heb. *called*   [y]Heb. *builded*
[z]Heb. *Isha*   [a]Heb. *Ish*

The fall of man

3 NOW [h]THE serpent was [i]more subtle than any beast of the field which the Lord God had made. And he said unto the woman, [b]Yea, hath God said, Ye shall not eat of every tree of the garden?

2 And the woman said unto the serpent, We may eat of the fruit of the trees of the garden:

3 But of the fruit of the tree which *is* in the midst of the garden, God hath said, Ye shall not eat of it, neither shall ye touch it, lest ye die.

4 [j]And the serpent said unto the woman, Ye shall not surely die:

5 For God doth know that in the day ye eat thereof, then your eyes shall be opened, and ye shall be as gods, knowing good and evil.

6 And when the woman saw that the tree *was* good for food, and that it *was* [c]pleasant to the eyes, and a tree to be desired to make *one* wise, she took of the fruit thereof, [k]and did eat, and gave also unto her husband with her; and he did eat.

7 And the eyes of them both were opened, [l]and they knew that they *were* naked; and they sewed fig leaves together, and made themselves [d]aprons.

8 And they heard [m]the voice of the Lord God walking in the garden in the [e]cool of the day: and Adam and his wife [n]hid themselves from the presence of the Lord God amongst the trees of the garden.

9 And the Lord God called Adam, and said unto him, Whe thou?

10 And he said, I heard thy v the garden, [o]and I was afrai cause I *was* naked; and I hid m

11 And he said, Who told the thou *wast* naked? Hast thou ea the tree, whereof I commande that thou shouldest not eat?

12 And the man said, [p]The w whom thou gavest *to be* with n gave me of the tree, and I did e

13 And the Lord God said un woman, What *is* this *that* tho done? And the woman said, [q]The serpent beguiled me, and I did eat.

14 And the Lord God said unto the serpent, Because thou hast done this, thou *art* cursed above all cattle, and above every beast of the field; upon thy belly shalt thou go, and [r]dust shalt thou eat all the days of thy life:

15 And I will put enmity between thee and the woman, and between [s]thy seed and [t]her seed; [u]it shall bruise thy head, and thou shalt bruise his heel.

16 Unto the woman he said, I will greatly multiply thy sorrow and thy conception; [v]in sorrow thou shalt bring forth children; [w]and thy desire *shall be* [f]to thy husband, and he shall [x]rule over thee.

17 And unto Adam he said, [y]Because thou hast hearkened unto the voice of thy wife, and hast eaten of the tree, [z]of which I commanded thee, saying, Thou shalt not eat of it: [a]cursed *is* the ground for thy sake; [b]in sorrow shalt thou eat *of* it all the days of thy life;

18 Thorns also and thistles shall it [g]bring forth to thee; and [c]thou shalt eat the herb of the field;

19 [d]In the sweat of thy face shalt thou eat bread, till thou return unto the ground; for out of it wast thou taken: [e]for dust thou *art*, and [f]unto dust shalt thou return.

20 And Adam called his wife's name [h]Eve; because she was the mother of all living.

21 Unto Adam also and to his wife did the Lord God make coats of skins, and clothed them.

22 And the Lord God said, Behold, the man is become as one of us, to know good and evil: and now, lest he put forth his hand, and take also of the tree of life, and eat, and live for ever:

23 Therefore the Lord God sent him forth from the garden of Eden, [g]to till the ground from whence he was taken.

24 So he drove out the man; and he placed [h]at the east of the garden of Eden [i]Cherubims, and a flaming sword which turned every way, to keep the way of the tree of life.

Cain and Abel

4 AND ADAM knew Eve his wife; eived, and bare ave gotten a man

bare his brother as [k]a keeper of as a tiller of the

s of time it came ought [j]of the fruit offering unto the

so brought of [k]the ck and of [l]the fat RD had [m]respect offering:

5 But unto Cain and to his offering he had not respect. And Cain was very wroth, [n]and his countenance fell.

6 And the Lord said unto Cain, Why art thou wroth? and why is thy countenance fallen?

7 If thou doest well, shalt thou not [n]be accepted? and if thou doest not well, sin lieth at the door. And [o]unto[o] thee *shall be* his desire, and thou shalt rule over him.

8 And Cain talked with Abel his

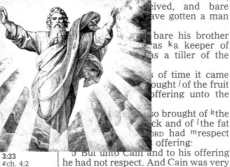

Cross references (center column)

3:1
[h]Rev. 12:9
[i]2 Cor. 11:3

3:4
[j]2 Cor. 11:3

3:6
[k]1 Tim. 2:14

3:7
[l]ch. 2:25

3:8
[m]Job 38:1
[n]Job 31:33
Jer. 23:24

3:10
[o]ch. 2:25
1 John 3:20

3:12
[p]Prov. 28:13

3:13
[q]ver. 4
2 Cor. 11:3
1 Tim. 2:14

3:14
[r]Is. 65:25

3:15
[s]John 8:44
Acts 13:10
1 John 3:8
[t]Is. 7:14
Luke 1:31,34,35
[u]Rom. 16:20
Rev. 12:7

3:16
[v]Is. 13:8
John 16:21

3:23
[g]ch. 4:2
& 9:20

3:24
[h]ch. 2:8
[i]Ps. 104:4
Heb. 1:7

4:3
[j]Num. 18:12

4:4
[k]Num. 18:17
[l]Lev. 3:16
[m]Heb. 11:4

4:5
[n]ch. 31:2

4:7
[o]ch. 3:16

Footnotes (bottom of right column)

[b]Heb. *Yea, because things to gird about*   [c]Heb. *a desire subject to thy husband*   [d]Or,   [e]Heb. *wind*   [g]Heb. *cause to bud*   [f]Or,   [h]Heb. *Chavah i.e. Living*   [i]i.e.Gotten   [j]Heb. *Hebel*   [k]Heb. *a feeder*   [l]Heb. *at the end of days*   [m]Heb. *sheep, or, goats*   [n]Or, *have the excellency?*   [o]Or, *subject unto thee,*

CHAPTER TWO

The Antiquity of Swearing

How old is swearing? It is as old as man and coeval with language. How old is man? Very near two million or more years.[1] And speech? ▇▇▇▇▇▇▇▇▇▇ it began at about the same time. Interestingly enough many philologists have held that speech originated in utterances closely akin to swearing. According to this theory,

spoken language began . . . when a cry of pain, formerly wrung out by real suffering, and seen to be understood and sympathized with, was repeated in imitation, no longer as a mere instinctive utterance, but for the purpose of intimating to another, "I am (was, shall be) suffering"; when an angry growl, formerly the direct expression of passion, was reproduced to signify disapprobation and threatening, and the like. This was enough to serve as a foundation for all that should be built upon it.[2]

William Dwight Whitney

AS OLD AS MAN AND SPEECH!

SO SWEARING
HAS BEEN
THERE FROM
THE BEGINNING
OF EVERYTHING.

Swearing, therefore, is prob-
ably coeval with the birth of language the sole or even the principal stimulus to the origin of speech.

So swearing is obviously old
as fuck and God started all this
but the boy was followed soon

WHEN EAR

HAD SOMETH

THEY SAID

THEIR HA

Y HUMANS

NG TO SAY,

WITH

DS.

GESTURE DEFINICTION

A MOVEMENT OR POSITION OF THE HAND, ARM, BODY, Head OR FACE THAT IS EXPRESSIVE OF AN IDEA, OPINION OR EMOTION. COMMUNICATING WITHOUT WORD.

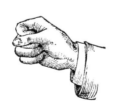

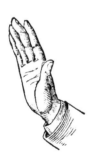

Negation:
This diagram
shows a hand
gesture that
represents
negation or
denial.

Determination:
This diagram
shows a hand
gesture that
represents
determination
or anger.

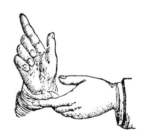

Argumentation
This diagram
shows a hand
gesture that
represents
argumentation.

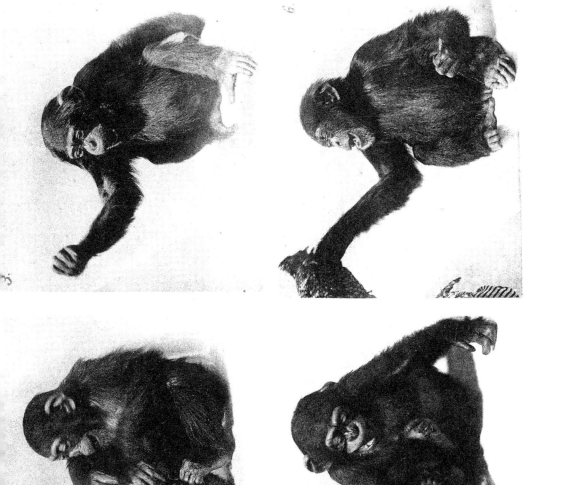

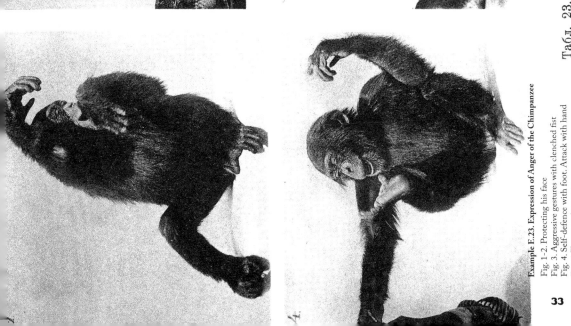

Example E.23. Expression of Anger of the Chimpanzee

Fig. 1-2. Protecting his face
Fig. 3. Aggressive gestures with clenched fist
Fig. 4. Self-defence with foot. Attack with hand
Fig. 5. Torturing his victim
Fig. 6. Pinching his victim

Табл. 23. Жесты защиты и нападения у шимпанзе.

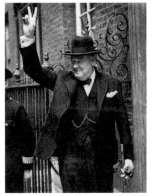

Winston Churchill,
British prime minister,
giving a hand gesture,
the V sign, for Victory
(photo taken in 1943)

Evolutionary anthropologists tell us that gesture is much older than speech. When early humans had something to say, they said it with their hands. And because manners didn't come along until a great deal later, it seems safe to assume that much of what people said was rude. Perhaps they wanted to disparage Og's performance in the bison hunt or the size of Bog's manhood. We don't know what signs they used, but we can be sure they used some.

By the time history was being recorded, its rude hand gestures were, too. Many of these are still in use today. Ancients insulted one another using many of the same gestures we use now, often with surprising gusto and frequency. In ancient Rome, the gesture popularly known as the Finger was so common that it even had a name: *digitus impudicus*.

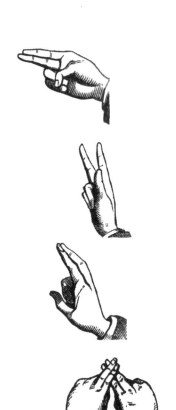

Over the next several thousand years, the language of hand gesture continued to evolve, with each region of the world developing its own colorful vocabulary of rude signs. These gestures express not just vulgar sentiments but deep truths about the culture itself. The insults a given culture favors are very revealing. Just as the Eskimos have many words for "snow," so the French have an infinite number of gestures to express ennui; the Lebanese, romantic desires; and the British, an urgent wish that you "piss off."

The language of hand signals continues to grow and change, with new gestures entering the vocabulary all the time. New gesturers enter as well. For most of history, hand gesturing—even the non-vulgar variety—was an almost exclusively male activity. Happily, in much of the world, that is no longer true, as more and more women proudly give the Bird.

Hand gestures point, quite literally, to where we've been and where we're going. They are especially relevant today. The advent of air travel means that one can find oneself in a distant country in a matter of hours and knowing not a single word.

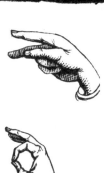
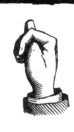
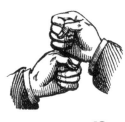
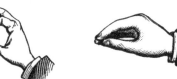
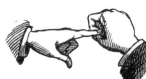

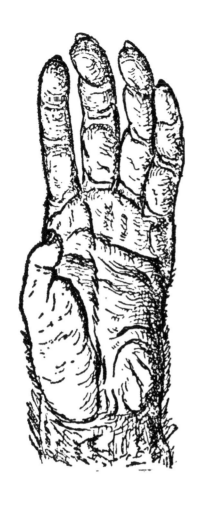

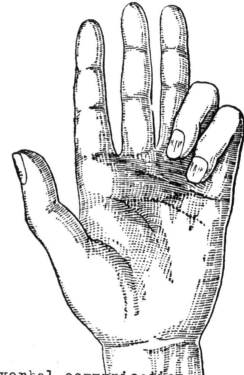

Gestures are part of nonverbal communication
That movement of the body or a part of it
that is expressive of thought or feeling.
There is evidendce to support that both
gestures and verbal language required for
effective learning. Gestures vafy depending
on the role in relation wo what is being said,
the role in relation to the situation, and the ~~~~~~~
cult ures in whichthey are used.

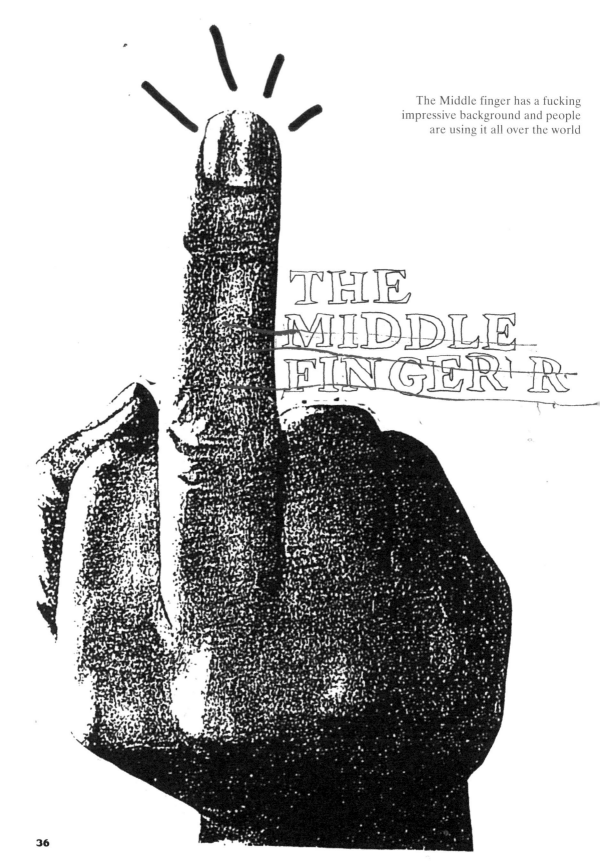

The Middle finger has a fucking impressive background and people are using it all over the world

THE MIDDLE FINGER R

In Western culture, the finger or the middle finger (as in giving someone the (middle) finger or the bird or flipping someone off,) is an obscene hand gesture. It communicates moderate to extreme contempt, and is roughly equivalent in meaning to „**fuck off**", „**fuck you**", „**shove it up your ass**", „**up yours**" or „**go fuck yourself**". It is performed by showing the back of a closed fist that has only the middle finger extended upwards, though in some locales the thumb is extended. Extending the finger is considered a symbol of contempt in several cultures, especially Western ones. Many cultures use similar gestures to display their disrespect, although others use it to express pointing without intentional disrespect toward other cultures.

The gesture dates back to Ancient Greece and it was also used in Ancient Rome. Historically, it represented the phallus. In some modern cultures, it has gained increasing recognition as a sign of disrespect, and has been used by music artists (notably more common among hardcore punk bands and rappers), actors, celebrities, athletes, and politicians. Most still view the gesture as obscene. The index finger and ring finger besides the middle finger in more contemporary periods has been likened to represent the testicles.

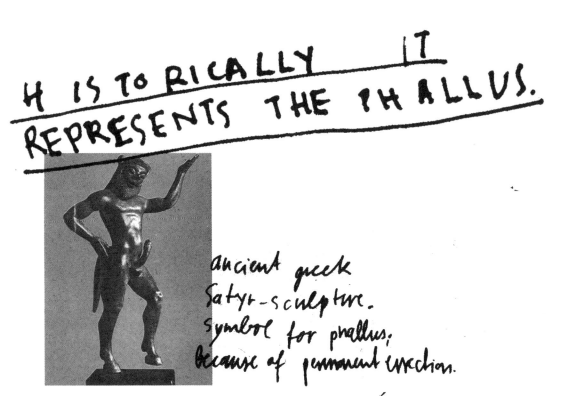

H IS TO RICALLY IT
REPRESENTS THE PHALLUS.

ancient greek
satyr-sculpture.
symbol for phallus;
because of permanent erection.

The origin
CLASSICAL ERA:

The middle finger gesture was used in Ancient times as a symbol of sexual intercourse, in a manner meant to degrade, intimidate and threaten the individual receiving the gesture. It also represented the phallus, with the fingers next to the middle finger representing testicles; from its close association, the gesture may have assumed apotropaic potency. In the 1st-century Mediterranean world, extending the finger was one of many methods used to divert the ever-present threat of the evil eye.

In Greek the gesture was known as the katapygon (κατάπυγον, from kata – κατά, „downwards" and pugē – πυγή, „rump, buttocks". In ancient Greek comedy, the finger was a gesture of insult toward another person, with the term katapugon also referring to „a male who submits to anal penetration" or katapygaina to a female. In Aristophanes's comedy The Clouds (423 BC),[14] when the character Socrates is quizzing his student on poetic meters, Strepsiades declares that he knows quite well what a dactyl is, and gives the finger. The gesture is a visual pun on the two meanings of the Greek word dactylos, both „finger" and the rhythmic measure composed of a long syllable and two short, like the joints of a finger (— ◡ ◡, which also appears as a visual pun on the penis and testicles in a medieval Latin text). Socrates reacts to the gesture as boorish and childish. The gesture recurs as a form of mockery in Peace, alongside farting in someone's face; the usage is later explained in the Suda and included in the Adagia of Erasmus. The verb „to play the Siphnian" appears in a fragment of Aristophanes and has a similar meaning; the usage is once again explained in the Suda, where it is said to mean „to touch the anus with a finger". Diogenes Laertius records how the Cynic philosopher Diogenes directed the gesture at the orator Demosthenes in 4th-century BC Athens.In the Discourses of Epictetus, Diogenes's target is instead one of the sophists.
In Latin, the middle finger was the digitus impudicus, meaning the „shameless, indecent or offensive finger". In the 1st century AD, Persius had superstitious female relatives concoct a charm with the „infamous finger" (digitus infamis) and „purifying spit";while in the Satyricon, an old woman uses dust, spit and her middle finger to mark the forehead before casting a spell. The poet Martial has a character in good health extend „the indecent one" toward three doctors. In another epigram, Martial wrote: „Laugh loud, Sextillus, at whoever calls you a cinaedus and extend your middle finger." Juvenal, through synecdoche, has the „middle nail" cocked at threatening Fortuna. The indecent finger features again in a mocking context in the Priapeia, a collection of poems relating to the phallic god Priapus.In Late Antiquity, the term „shameless finger" is explained in the Etymologiae of Isidore of Seville with reference to its frequent use when accusing someone of a „shameful action".

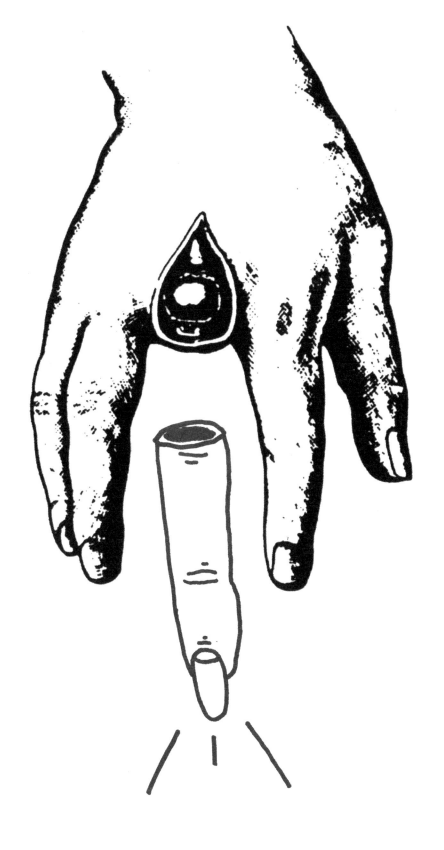

CHARLES's CASUAL FUCK YOU.

CHARLES "OLD HOSS" RADBOURN (TOP LEFT IN THE PHOTOGRAPH) WAS A BASEBALL PITCHER FOR THE BOSTON BEANEATERS. HE WAS THE FIRST DOCUMENTED PUBLIC FIGURE PHOTOGRAPHED (1886) "GIVING THE FINGER." HE GAVE IT TO THEIR RIVALS, THE NEW YORK GIANTS BEFORE THE GAME.

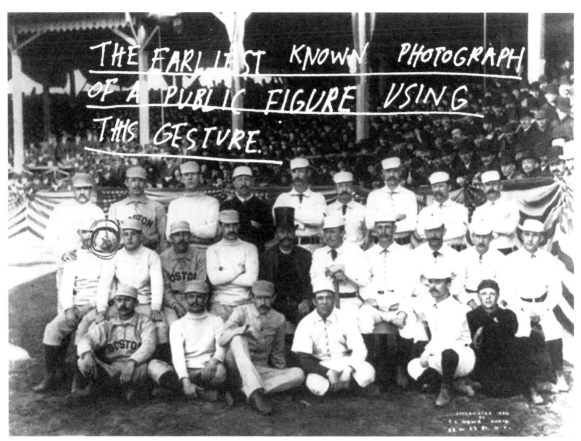

The baseball pitcher Charles Radbourn was the first documented public figure giving the finger (1886)

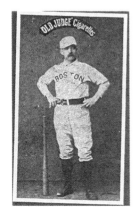

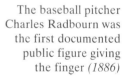

CHARLES "OLD HOSS" RADBOURN REPEATED HIS "CASUAL FUCK YOU" IN HIS PLAYER CARD OF 1887

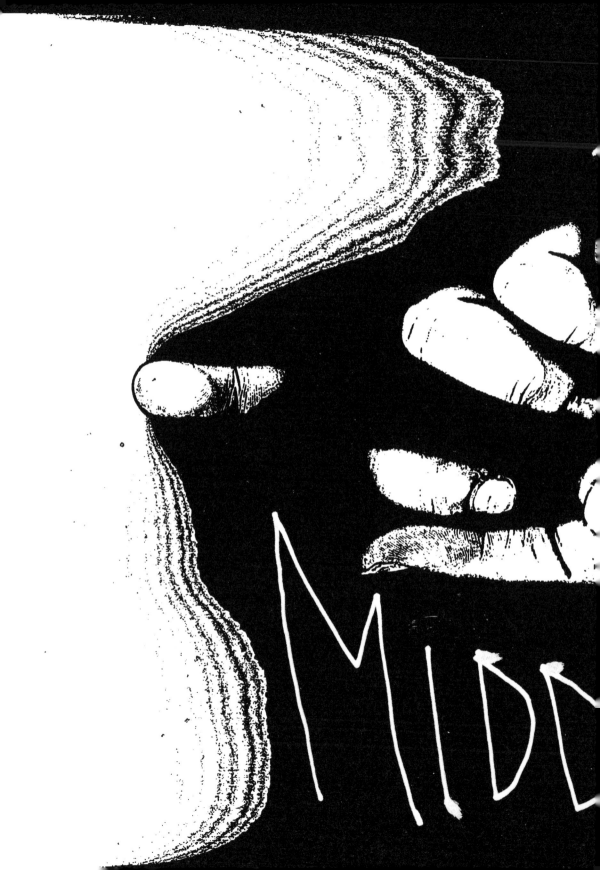

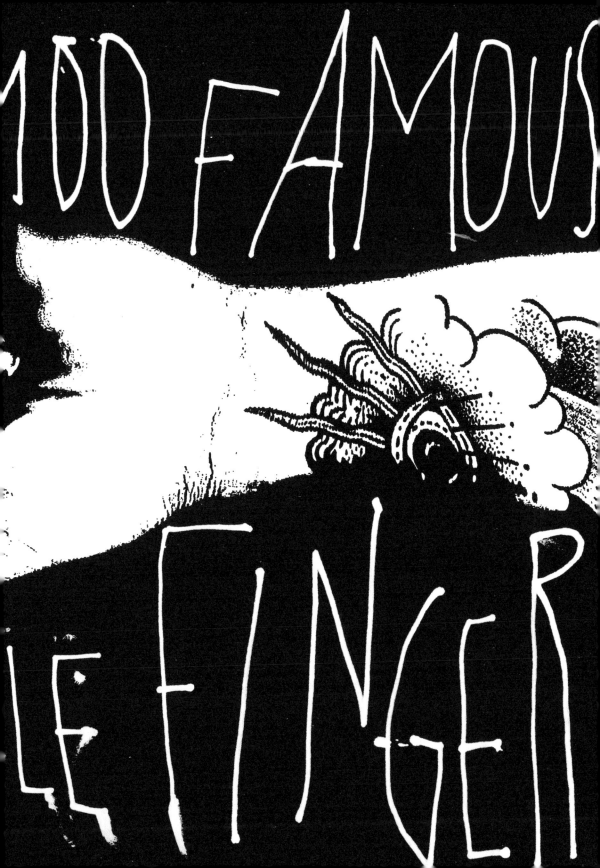

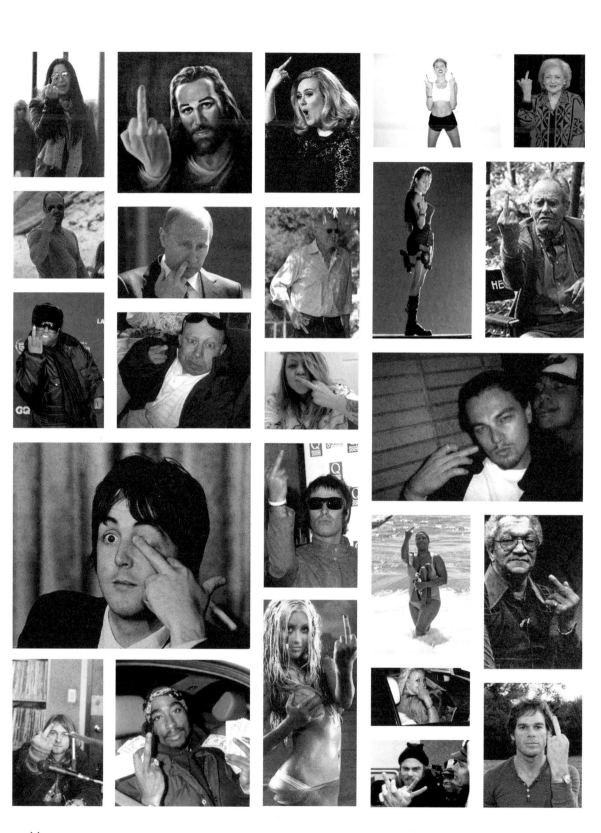

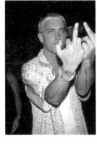
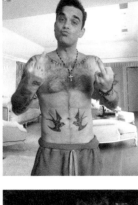
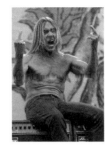
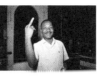
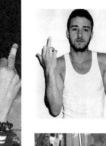

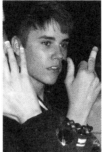
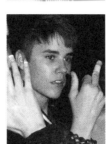
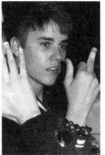
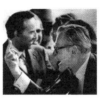
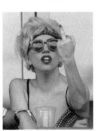
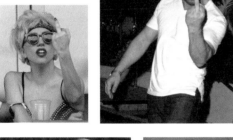
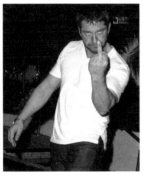
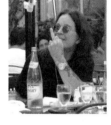
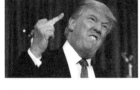
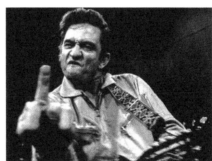
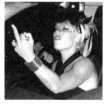
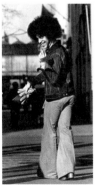
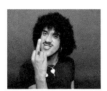
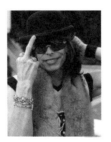
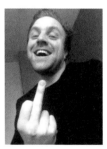
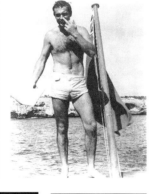
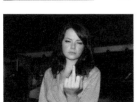
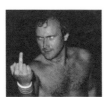
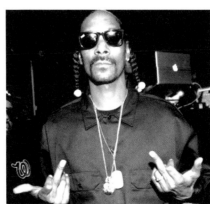
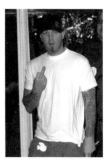

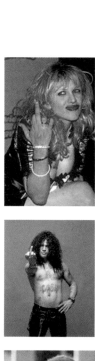
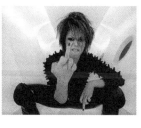
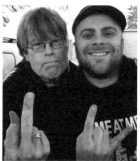
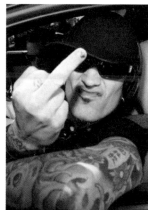
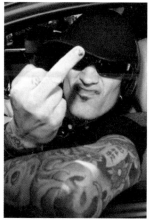
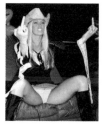
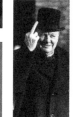
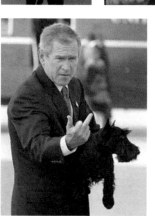
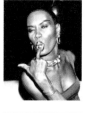
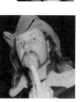
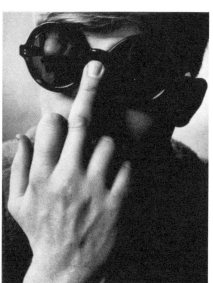
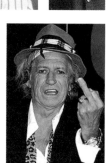
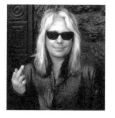
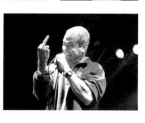
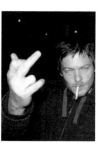
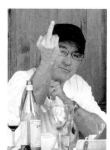
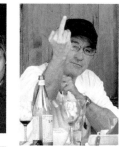
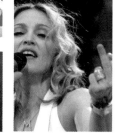
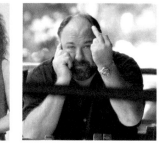
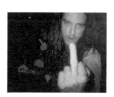

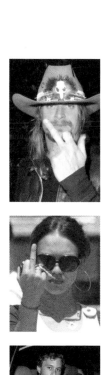
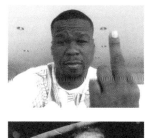
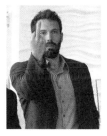
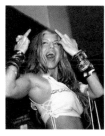
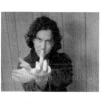
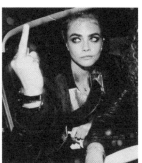
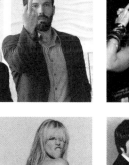
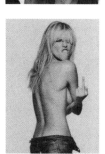
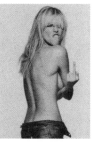
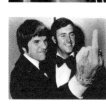
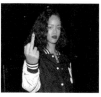
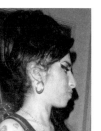
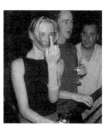
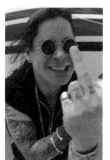
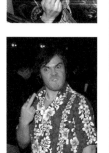
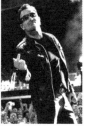
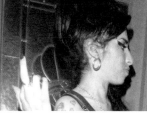

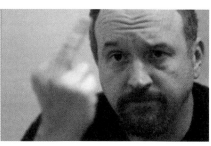
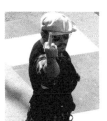
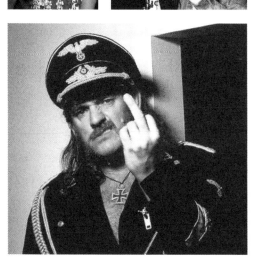
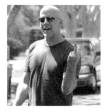
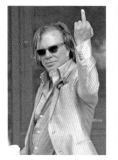
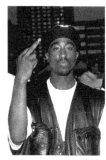
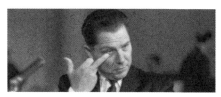

More offensive hand gestures from all over the world...

THE CONCHA

Meaning: Your mother has dried-up lady parts
Used in: Chile, Argentina.

In most of the world, this gesture simply means "hungry," but in Chile and Argentina, it means something quite different. This rather offensive gesture is short for *concha de tu madre* and refers to the "shell"—or love canal—of the subject's mother. The insult further implies that it is not a well-watered canal at all, but a dry riverbed.

WANKER

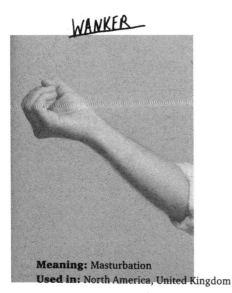

Meaning: Masturbation
Used in: North America, United Kingdom

In this coarse and explicit gesture, the hand is jerked repeatedly in a pantomime of male self-pleasure. The implication is that the subject is so hopeless that masturbation is his only recourse to sexual satisfaction. Its natural habitat is the football arena, where it is often employed by fans against the opposing team.

CHIN FLICK

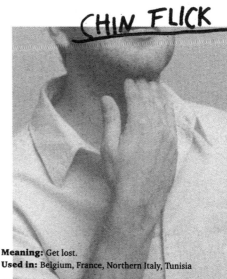

Meaning: Get lost.
Used in: Belgium, France, Northern Italy, Tunisia

In France, this gesture is known as *la barbe*, or "the beard," the idea being that the gesturer is flashing his masculinity in much the same way that a buck will brandish his horns or a cock his comb. Simply brush the hand under the chin in a forward flicking motion. While not as aggressive as flashing one's actual genitalia, this gesture is legal and remains effective as a mildly insulting brush-off.

NOTE: In Italy, this gesture simply means "No."

FODEU

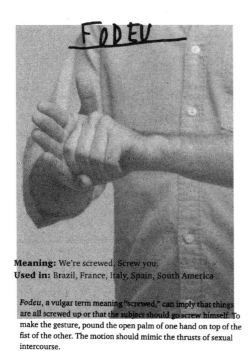

Meaning: We're screwed. Screw you.
Used in: Brazil, France, Italy, Spain, South America

Fodeu, a vulgar term meaning "screwed," can imply that things are all screwed up or that the subject should go screw himself. To make the gesture, pound the open palm of one hand on top of the fist of the other. The motion should mimic the thrusts of sexual intercourse.

HUEVON

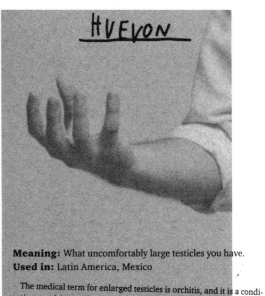

Meaning: What uncomfortably large testicles you have.
Used in: Latin America, Mexico

The medical term for enlarged testicles is orchitis, and it is a condition requiring medical attention. Here the suggestion is not that the subject may be ill, but that his oversized genitalia are making him lazy and, perhaps, rendering him undesirable to women. To make the gesture, which is used only between men, simply cup a palm upward, as if holding something heavy. Medical attention is not required, but an apology may be.

MOUTZA

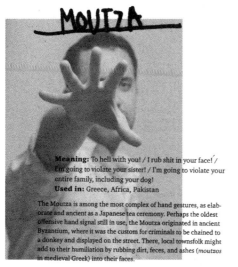

Meaning: To hell with you! / I rub shit in your face! / I'm going to violate your sister! / I'm going to violate your entire family, including your dog!
Used in: Greece, Africa, Pakistan

The Moutza is among the most complex of hand gestures, as elaborate and ancient as a Japanese tea ceremony. Perhaps the oldest offensive hand signal still in use, the Moutza originated in ancient Byzantium, where it was the custom for criminals to be chained to a donkey and displayed on the street. There, local townsfolk might add to their humiliation by rubbing dirt, feces, and ashes (*moutzos* in medieval Greek) into their faces.

Now that the advent of modern sewage systems and antismoking laws means that these materials are no longer readily available, the Moutza is a symbolic stand-in. In Greece, it is often accompanied by commands including *par'ta* ("take these") or *órse* ("there you go"). Over the years, the versatile Moutza has acquired more connotations, including a sexual one, in which the five extended fingers suggest the five sexual acts the gesturer would like to perform with the subject's willing sister.

The Moutza has many variations, each appropriate to its own occasion. See variations on the following pages.

FIG

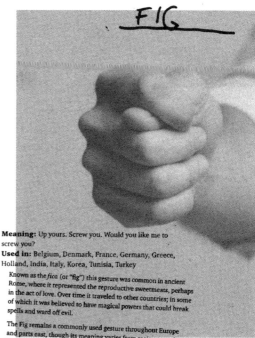

Meaning: Up yours. Screw you. Would you like me to screw you?
Used in: Belgium, Denmark, France, Germany, Greece, Holland, India, Italy, Korea, Tunisia, Turkey

Known as the *fica* (or "fig") this gesture was common in ancient Rome, where it represented the reproductive sweetmeats, perhaps in the act of love. Over time it traveled to other countries; in some of which it was believed to have magical powers that could break spells and ward off evil.

The Fig remains a commonly used gesture throughout Europe and parts east, though its meaning varies from region to region. In some, it retains its original sexual connotation; in others, it is a good luck gesture meant to dispel bad fortune; and in still others, it is a profane insult. To execute, simply make a fist with the thumb protruding between the index and middle finger. Given the Fig's widely varying meanings, the savvy traveler will avoid playing "got your nose" with his host's children, lest an extremely awkward reaction result.

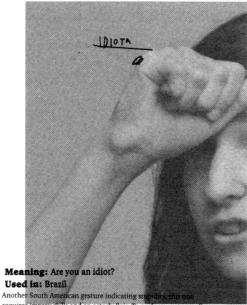

Meaning: Are you an idiot?
Used in: Brazil

Another South American gesture indicating stupidity, this one requires improv skills and an actorly flair. To perform, put your fist to your forehead while making a comical overbite. The gesture is most effective when accented with multiple grunts of arrr, arrr. When executed correctly, you will be rewarded with appreciative laughs, though not, perhaps, from your subject.

ON SE TIRE

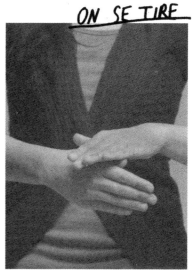

Meaning: Get lost.
Used in: France, Belgium, Greece, Italy, Spain, Tunisia, Yugoslavia

In this gesture of dismissal, the left hand chops or clamps down on the right wrist, forcing the right hand to flick up. The chopping motion mimics the severing of a thief's hand and tells the subject he deserves to be banished like a common bandit. The gesture can also be used without insulting intent to signify "Let's go."

CORNA

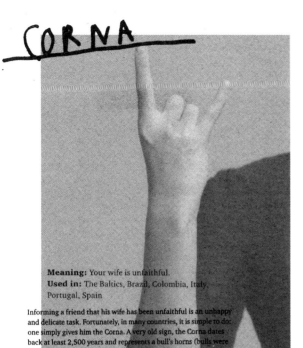

Meaning: Your wife is unfaithful.
Used in: The Baltics, Brazil, Colombia, Italy, Portugal, Spain

Informing a friend that his wife has been unfaithful is an unhappy and delicate task. Fortunately, in many countries, it is simple to do: one simply gives him the Corna. A very old sign, the Corna dates back at least 2,500 years and represents a bull's horns (bulls were commonly castrated to make them calmer).

Be warned that while the gesture is used throughout the world, its meaning varies greatly from country to country. In many countries, it is simply an expression of good luck; in others, it demonstrates an affection for a certain sporting team or musical group. Should you be on the receiving end of the gesture, before you cast out your wife, remember that your pal may simply be saying she is a fan of American college football or heavy metal bands.

DONKEY RIDE

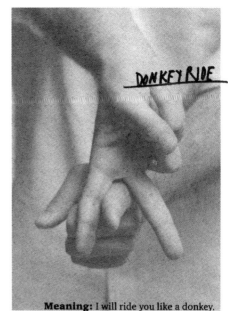

Meaning: I will ride you like a donkey.
Used in: Saudi Arabia

An elaborate two-handed gesture, this sign is like a puppet show in which the fingers act out an intricate maneuver whose message is "I will ride you like a donkey." To make the gesture, form an upside-down V (representing the rider's legs) with the first two fingers of your right hand and then straddle the left forefinger (representing the donkey). Orchestrating this gesture does not take much less effort than actually mounting the subject, but it is considerably less awkward.

QUEEN ANNE'S FAN

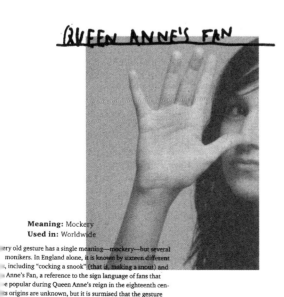

Meaning: Mockery
Used in: Worldwide

...ery old gesture has a single meaning—mockery—but several monikers. In England alone, it is known by sixteen different ..., including "cocking a snook" (that is, making a snout) and ...Anne's Fan, a reference to the sign language of fans that ...e popular during Queen Anne's reign in the eighteenth cen-...'s origins are unknown, but it is surmised that the gesture ...nt to mimic a deformed nose or a cock's comb. The insult it ...'s is mild and playful. For added whimsy, waggle the fingers ...up the second hand behind the first.

FIVE FATHERS

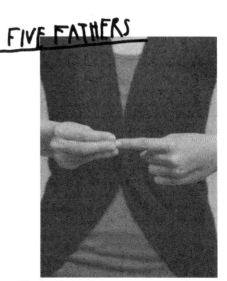

Meaning: You have five fathers, i.e., your mother is a whore.
Used in: Arab countries, Caribbean

If you are looking to get yourself deported from Saudi Arabia—possibly amid a riot—you can do no better than the Five Fathers gesture. The most inflammatory hand gesture in the Arab world, this sign accuses the subject's mother of cavorting with every Tom, Dick, and Mustafa, implying that she had so many suitors that paternity is impossible to determine. To execute, point your left index finger at your right hand, while pursing all fingers of the right hand together. The insult is extreme and almost certain to provoke violence.

SWEAR
IS A FO
EMOTIC
EXPRES

ING

RM OF

ONAL

SION

WHATEVER WE DO IS
NOTHING LESS THAN
EXPRESSION.

WE DREAM, PAINT, SING, DANCE, ~~SCALE~~ SOCIALIZE
EAT, TALK, BLOG, FIGHT, KILL, LOVE,
~~####~~ FUCK, SING, DRINK AND WE

SWEAR

The act of making
your thoughts, feelings,
etc. known by speech,
writing, or any other
method is called the act
of expressing something

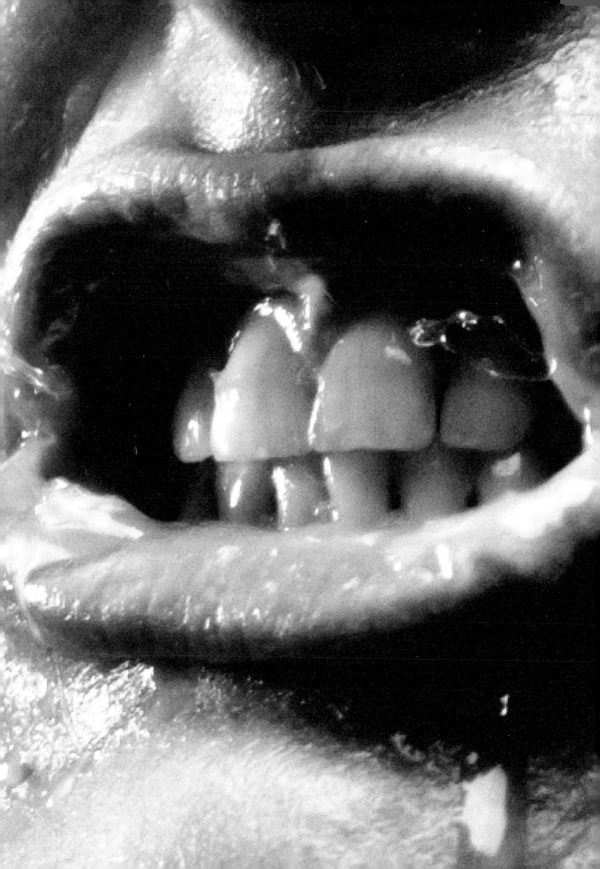

EXPRESS

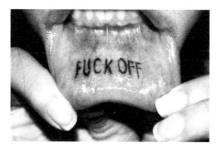

YOURSELF

Swearing is a strong way to express yourself and there are tons of ways to fucking do this

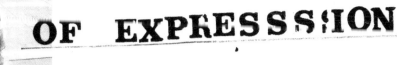

MORE FORMS OF EXPRESSSION

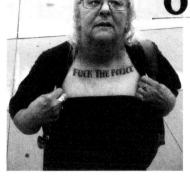

We already found out that swearing
is obviously all over the place .
Humans use it as a tool in many different
ways since forever . In movies, art, comedy
But there is of course more than that,
We use strong curse words to portray our
deepemotional investment in a personal
identi identity. To show what we think, feel or
what's our opinion on things or persons.
We differentiate ourselves from others
often with the way we dress, or how we look
like. So usin swearin as a way to express ourselfs
comes to next level when we display it on our bodies
as tattoos or in fashion.
 We use swear words because the way we handle them
in society has make them strong.ximusi
Censorship, taboos and the idea of swearing
being a dirty thing, all t hose facts makex
are the reason why curse words feel so powerfull.

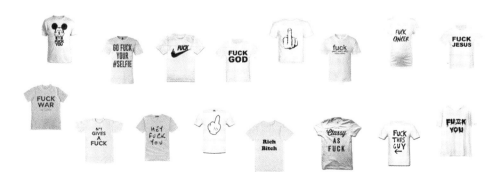

HOW HAS SWEARING EVOLVED?

IN THEIR JOURNEY AS SOLITARY HUNTERS, PREHISTORIC HUMANS REALIZED THE OBVIOUS ADVANTAGE OF HUNTING IN PACKS. THIS REQUIRED THEM TO COME UP WITH TACTICS, TO LEARN SKILLS AND TO EXECUTE COORDINATION. THE ABILITY TO EXPRESS AND TO UNDERSTAND OTHERS IN A GROUP BECAME MORE ~~REQU~~ OF A REQUIREMENT TO SURVIVE.

THE GROUPS OF HUMANS WHO COULD DO THIS HAD
A BETTER CHANCE OF SURVIVAL. SOON GROUPS
ENVOLVED INTO TRIBES, THEN INTO CULTURES
AND THEN INTO CIVILIZATIONS. THIS IS
THE PATH THAT LED HUMANS TO EVOLVE
INTO THE SOCIAL BEINGS WE ARE TODAY.
         LIVING IN GROUPS HAD ITS OWN
PROBLEMS. THE GROUP PERFORMED AS ONE
UNIT BUT WAS DIVIDED INTO INDIVIDUALS WITH
DIFFERENT GENETIC MAKE UPS. ONE STRING
THAT COULD CONNECT DIFFERENT INDIVIDUALS
TOGETHER WAS THEIR ABILITY TO EXPRESS AND
UNDERSTAND. THIS IS THE REASON WHY
WE LONG TO EXPRESS AND BE UNDERSTOOD.
ART, MUSIC, DANCE, DRAMA, LANGUAGE ARE MEDIUMS
THAT HAVE HELPED US PROJECT WHAT'S INSIDE
OUR MINDS. SO DID SWEARING. WE WERE ABLE
TO EXPRESS LOVE AND AT THE SAME TIME
HATE — JUST WITH THE POWER OF SWEARING AS
A WAY OF EASY COMMUNICATION.

FUCK
YOU

THE BREAK OUT OF SWEARING
THE FIRST ONE THROUGH
THE WALL GETS A...... BLOODY

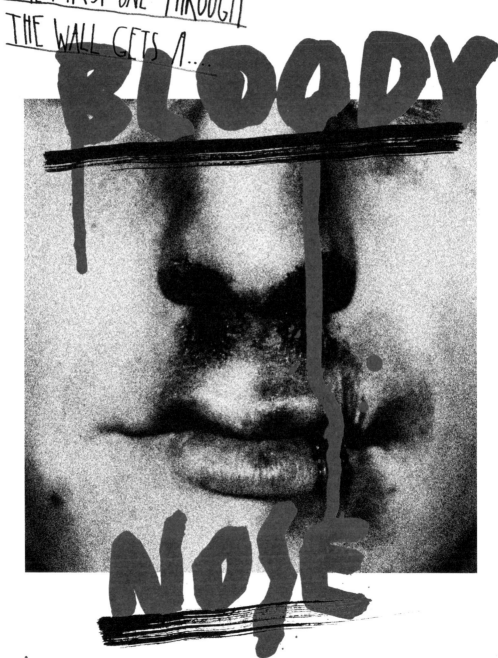

NOSE

FOR CENTURIES
SWEARING WAS BANNED,
CENSORED & AVOIDED.
IT WASN'T USED ACROSS
FILM, TELEVISION
AND MUSIC.

all until one man!

GEORGE CARLIN

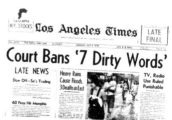

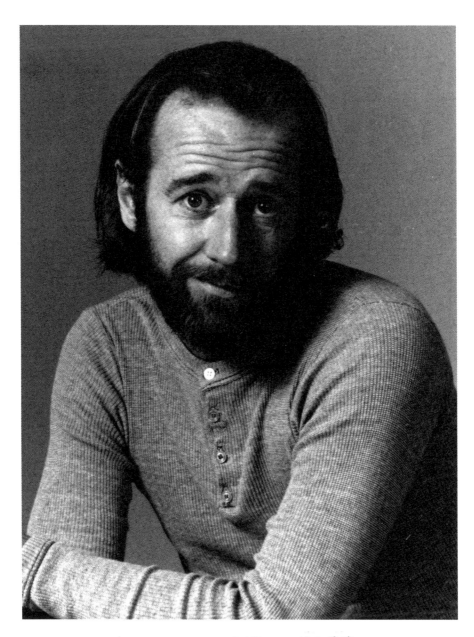

"(...) It's not a science. It's a notion that
they have and it' SUPERSTITIOUS. These words
have NO POWER. We give them this power by refusing
to be free and easy with them.
WE GIVE THEM GREAT POWER OVER US. They really, in
themselves, have no power at all. It's the
thrus t of the sentence that makes them either good
or bad." CARLIN, 2004

SHIT

PISS

FUCK

CUNT

TITS

COCKSUCKER

MOTHERFUCKER

At the time, the words were considered highly inappropriate and unsuitable for broadcast on the public airwaves in the United States, whether radio or television. As such, they were avoided in scripted material, and bleep censored in the rare cases in which they were used; broadcast standards differ in different parts of the world, then and now, although most of the words on Carlin's original list remain taboo on American broadcast television as of 2016. The list was not an official enumeration of forbidden words, but rather was compiled by Carlin. Nonetheless, a radio broadcast featuring these words led to a U.S. Supreme Court decision that helped establish the extent to which the federal government could regulate speech on broadcast television and radio in the United States.

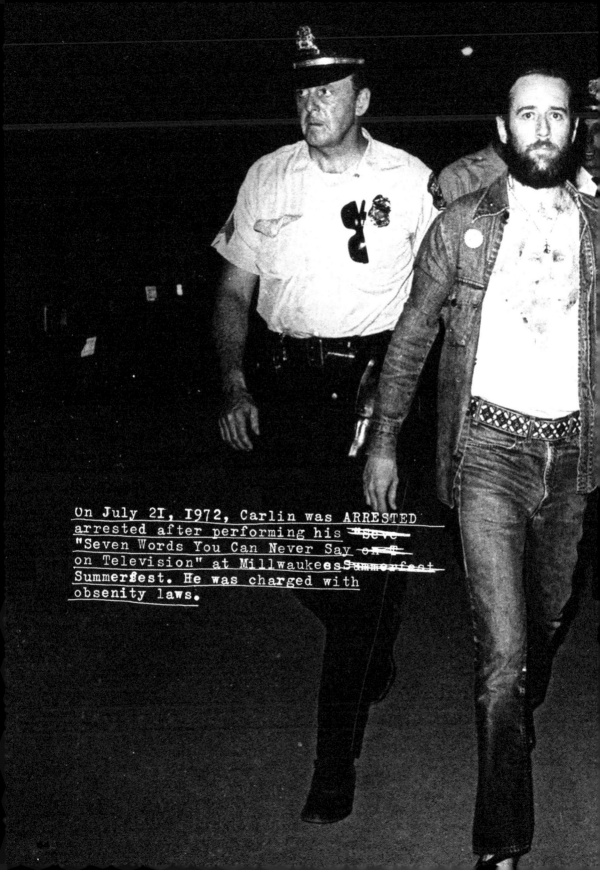

On July 2I, I972, Carlin was ARRESTED
arrested after performing his ~~seve~~
"Seven Words You Can Never Say ~~on T~~
on Television" at Millwaukees ~~Summerfest~~
Summerfest. He was charged with
obsenity laws.

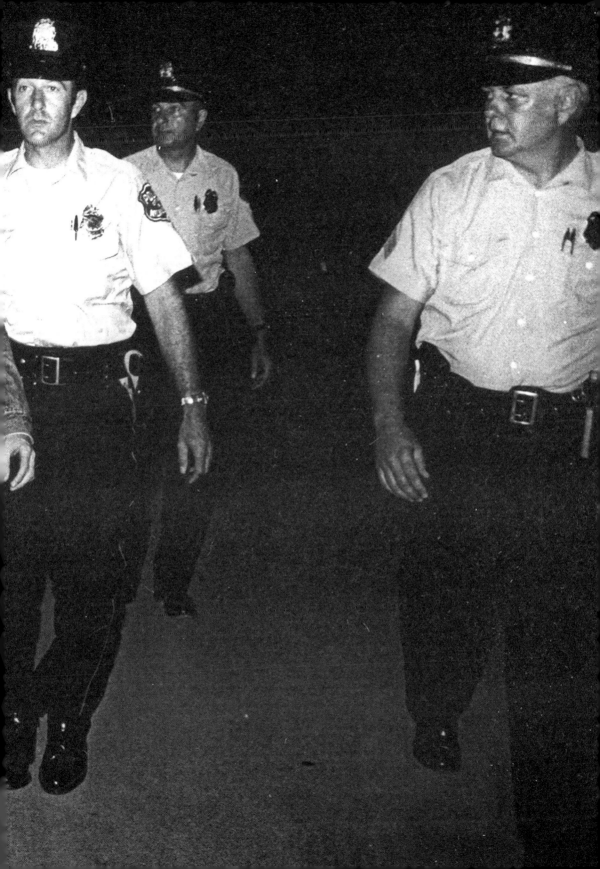

Censorship in Music & the PARENTS MUSIC RESOURE CENTER (PMRC)

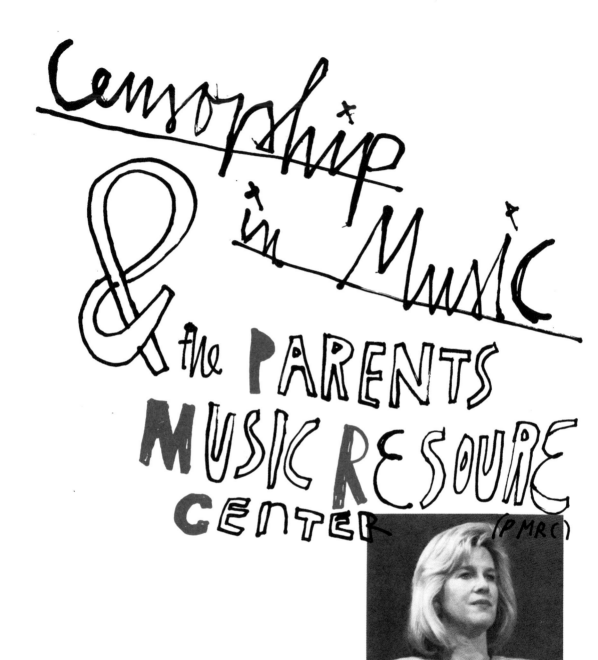

The source of all artists problems:
Tipper Gore, wife of Senator *Al Gore*
and leader of the *PMRC* gang

THE PARENTS MUSIC RESOURCE CENTER (PMRC)
WAS AN AMERICAN COMMITTEE FORMED IN
1985 WITH THE STATED GOAL OF INCREASING
PARENTAL CONTROL OVER THE ACCESS OF
CHILDREN TO MUSIC DEEMED TO HAVE VIOLENT,
DRUG-RELATED OR SEXUAL THEMES VIA
LABELING ALBUMS WITH PARENTAL ADVISORY
STICKERS. THE COMMITTEE WAS FOUNDED
BY FOUR WOMEN: TIPPER GORE, WIFE OF
SENATOR AL GORE; SUSAN BAKER, WIFE OF
TREASURY SECRETARY JAMES BAKER; PAM
HOWAR, WIFE OF WASHINGTON REALTOR
RAYMOND HOWAR AND SALLY NEVIUS,
WIFE OF FORMER WASHINGTON CITY
COUNCIL CHAIRMAN JOHN NEVIUS.
THEY WERE KNOWEN AS THE
"WASHINGTON WIVES"- A REFERENCE
TO THEIR HUSBANDS' CONNECTIONS
WITH THE GOVERNMENT.

-The- Washington WIFES

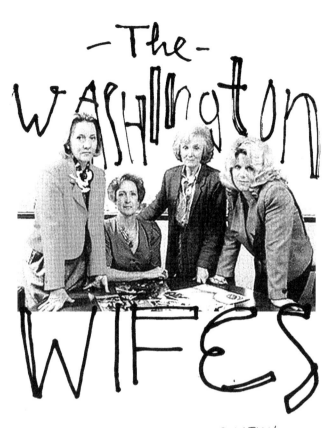

The Filthy Fifteen

ARTIST	SONG	RATING*
JUDAS PRIEST	"Eat Me Alive"	X
MÖTLEY CRÜE	"Bastard"	V
PRINCE	"Darling Nikki"	X
SHEENA EASTON	"Sugar Walls"	X
W.A.S.P.	"(Animal) Fuck Like a Beast"	X
MERCYFUL FATE	"Into the Coven"	O
VANITY	"Strap On Robby Baby"	X
DEF LEPPARD	"High 'n' Dry"	D/A
TWISTED SISTER	"We're Not Gonna Take It"	V
MADONNA	"Dress You Up"	X
CYNDI LAUPER	"She Bop"	X
AC/DC	"Let Me Put My Love into You"	X
BLACK SABBATH	"Trashed"	D/A
MARY JANE GIRLS	"My House"	X
VENOM	"Possessed"	O

*(Proposed)   X = Profane or sexually explicit   O = Occult   D-A = Drugs or alcohol   V = Violent

SHORTLY AFTER THEIR FORMATION
IN APRIL 1985, THE WIFES ASSEMBLED
A LIST OF FIFTEEN SONGS WITH DEEMED
UNSUITABLE CONTENT. IT WAS THE TOP
FIFTEEN SONGS RECOMMENDED TO BE
BANNED, AND THEIR PRESUMED SUBJECT MATTER.
THE RECORDING INDUSTRY ASSOCIATION (RIAA)
RESPONDED BY INTRODUCING AN EARLY VERSION
OF THE PARENTAL ADVISORY LABEL. IT ALL
WENT TO COURT - NOTABLE MUSICIANS, LIKE
FRANK ZAPPA OR JOHN DENVER WERE TESTIFIED
AT THIS HEARING WITH STRONG OPPOSITION
TO PMRC'S WARNING LABEL SYSTEM AND
CENSORSHIP IN GENERAL - BUT COURT
DECIDED: AUDIO RECORDINGS WERE FROM
NOW ON EITHER BE AFFIXED WITH THE
"WARNING"STICKER PARENTAL ADVISORY OR
HAVE ITS LYRICS ATTACHED ON THE
BACKSIDE OF ITS PACKAGING.

many MUSICIANS have CRITICIZED and PARODIED tHE PMRC and ESPECIALLY TIPPERGORE

Some Examples:
(John Lydon, NOFX, Danzig, Megadeath, Ice-T, Eminem
Warrant, Sonic Youth, Anthrax, Rage against the machine
Ozzy Osbourne, Frank Zappa, The Ramones, Dead Kennedys
and many more........)

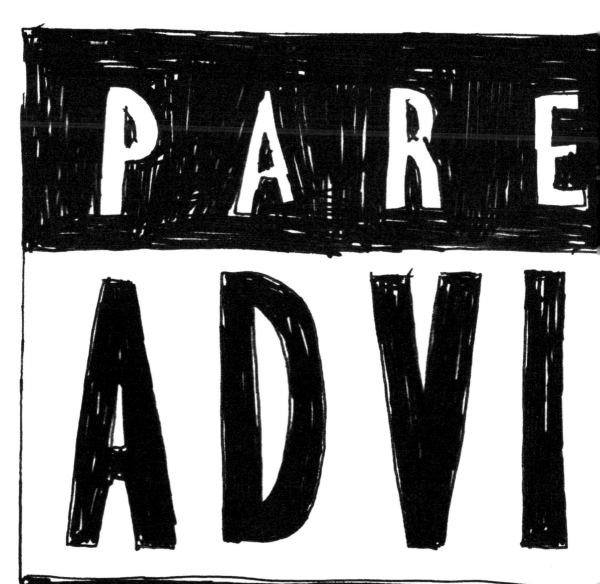

NTAL
SORY
CONTENT

FOLLOWED BY
PPROTESTS
& reactions of
different artist

COLOSSAL WASSAIL RECORDS PRESENTS

NOFX
NOFX

"THE PMRC
CAN SUCK
ON THIS" EP

FAT

1987 NOFX RELEASED AN EP TITLED
The P.M.R.C. CAN SUCK ON THIS.

1788 DANZIG'S SONG "Mother" scored a TOP 40 HIT.
IT'S THE MOST FAMOUS SONG ABOUT the PMRC.
IT'S STILL ONE OF THE ONLY SONGS ABOUT
TIPPER GORE & PMRC

1989 ICE-T ALBUM "THE ICEBERG-FREEDOM OF SPEECH.
HAD ONE PARTICULAR SONG ON IT THAT WAS AN
EXTEND ATTACK TO TIPPER GORE

1992 the RAMONES recorded THE song ALBUM "CENSORSHIT"

1992 THE RAMONES RECORDED THE SONG "CENSORSHIT"
ABOUT HOW ROCK AND RAP ALBUMS ARE BEING CENSORED
BY THE PMRC.(AGAIN ADRESSED TO GORE)

Tipper, what's that sticker sticking on my CD?
Is that some kind of warning to protect me?
Freedom of choice needs a stronger, stronger voice.
You can stamp out the source, but you
Can't stop creative thoughts.
(RAMONES "CENSORSHIT" LYRICS)

ICE T- freedom of Speech

»YO TIP, WHAT'S the matter? YOU AIN'T GETTIN NO DICK? YOU'RE BITCHING ABOUT ROCK 'n ROLL! That is Censorship - DUMP BITCH!

Artists are still cussing, now more than ever. There's much hate against *Tipper Gore* and she actually gave them another reason to swear

WHEN DID SWEARI IN MOVIE

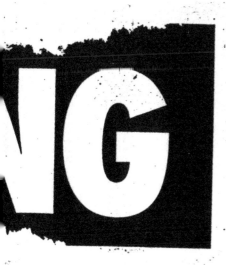

NG

S

START?

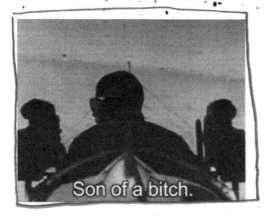

Swearing is something we're barely aware of in movies these days but it used to be taken fucking seriously

TODAY

HISTORY OF IS SWEARING IN MOVIES

Movies tend to avoid profanity.
There are R-rated movies.

1983 AL PACINO broke the record for saying
FUCK the most times in film history
in the movie Scarface

1971 JACK NICHOLSON became the first A-list
actor to swear on camera (in the movie:
Carnal Knowledge with the line:
ANSWER ME YOU BALLBURSTING CASTRATING
SON OF A CUNT BITCH)

1970 The movie "MASH" became the first
Hollywood movie to use the word "fuxk"

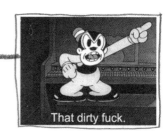
That dirty fuck.

1968 Motion Picture Association of
America decided to lift the ban on
swearwords.

1939 Gone with the wind broke that ban
by using the word "DAMN" . The producers
ended up paying a 85.000Dollar fine for
using it.

1934 Motion Picture Association
of America decided to ban profanity

1929 First

1929 First use of the word "DAMN"

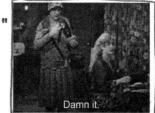
Damn it.

BACK THEN

76

"ANSWER ME YOU BALLBUSTING CASTRATING SON OF A CUNT BITCH"

Swearing is something we're barely aware
of in movies these days - but it used to be
taken a lot more seriously. Filmmakers embraced the joys
of pxx PROFANITY in the early 30s.
However,there was a time when th e Motion Picture
Association Of America banned the use of profanity
in moviessx and the use of swear words was met with a fine.
Nowadays we have filmmakers like QUENTIN TARAnTINO or
MARTIN SCORSESE who use profanity rather **liberally**
and effectively.

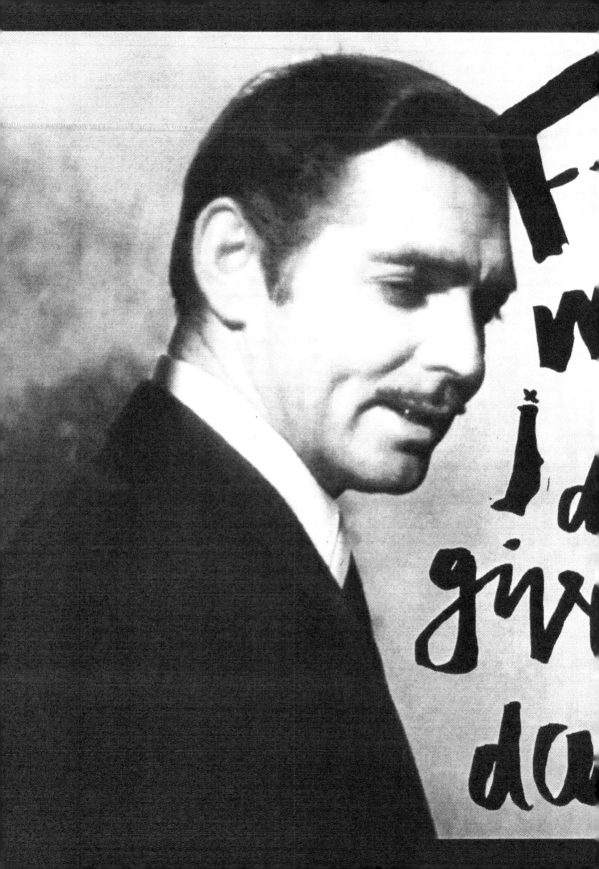

rankly

y dear,

n't

a

nn!

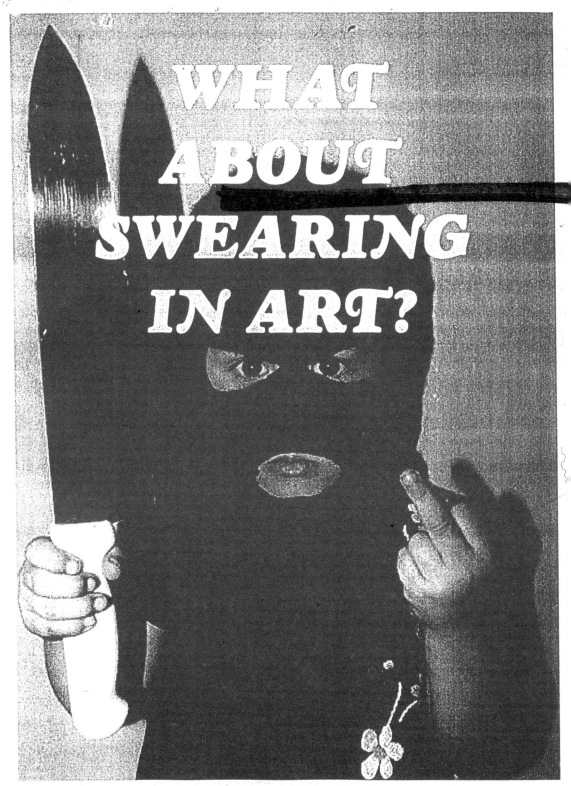

WHAT ABOUT SWEARING IN ART?

Swearing has been and still is used as a powerful tool in art and media, this shows the power of swear words and rude gestures again, the more we try to ban them the stronger they'll get

OF COURSE THERE IS

ALSO SWEARING IN ART

SOME EXAMPLES WILL FOLLOW

ON THE NEXT PAGES

SIDENOTE: Putin signed alaw in
2014 that banns Curse
Words in Arts (and media)
The words khuy(cock), pizda(cunt)
~~and blyad (who~~
and blyad (whore) – a smutty
quartet known as mat-will be
banned. Violators of the law
face fines of between 70dollars
an 1,400dollar.

STUDY OF PERSPEC

THE SARDONIC HUMOR OF AI WEIWEI'S "STUDY OF PERSPECTIVE" SERIES BELIES A POWERFUL PROTESTATION BEHIND THE GESTURE, A REJECTION OF THE POWER HELD BY CULTURE AND POLITICS, AND REBELLION AGAINST AUTHORITY. THIS IS ONE OF AI WEIWEI'S MOST CONTROVERSIAL SERIES, PHOTOGRAPHING HIMSELF RAISING HIS MIDDLE FINGER TOWARD TIANANMEN SQUARE, THE WHITE HOUSE, THE EIFFEL TOWER, AND OTHER NOTABLE LANDMARKS AROUND THE WORLD. ~~THIS PERSPECTIVE THROUGH~~

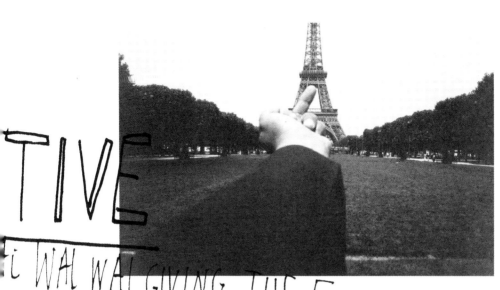

TIVE

E WAI WAI GIVING THE FINGER
TO THE WORLDS AUTHORITIES.

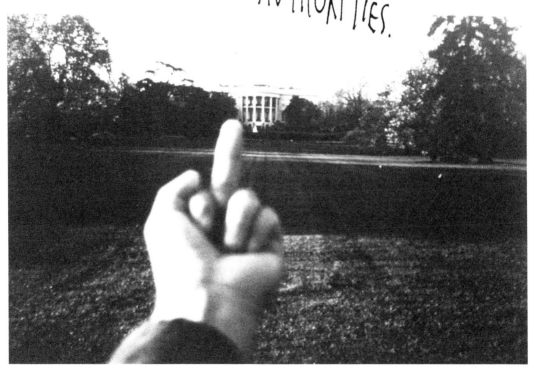

THIS SCULPTURE IS GIVING A GIANT FUCK YOU TO THE CZECH PRESIDENT

CONTROVERSIAL CZECH ARTIST DAVID CERNY, KNOWN FOR HIS ANTI-COMMUNIST STANCE, HAS SENT A VERY CLEAR MESSAGE TO THE REPUBLIC'S PRESIDENT AHEAD OF PARLIAMENTARY POLLS BY INSTALLING A GIANT (10 METER HIGH) PURPLE HAND WITH A RAISED MIDDLE FINGER ON PRAGUES MAIN RIVER. THE HUGE FINGER IS FLOATING NEAR THE CHARLES BRIDGE AND IS POINTED AT THE PRAGUE CASTLE — THE SEAT OF PRESIDENT MILOS ZEMAN.

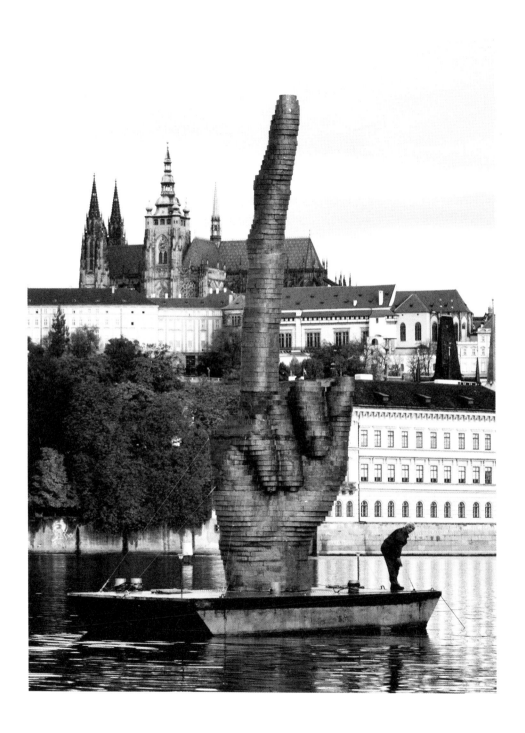

MAURICIO CATTELAN'S

L. O. V. E.

SCULPTURE IN FRONT OF THE MILAN STOCK EXCHANGE.

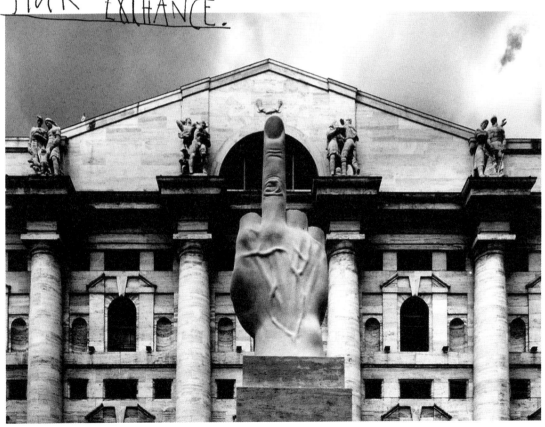

CATTELAN MADE A RUDE STATEMENT

WHY NOT? WALL STREET

HAS A `BULL`!

~~SO NOW~~

THE INSTALLATION HAS FUELLED CRITICISM
AMONG LOCAL POLITICIANS AND
INTELLECTUALS OVER THE RIGHTS
AND WRONGS OF SHOWING A PROVOCATIVE
WORK IN A PUBLIC SPACE. ASKED
ABOUT THE MEANING OF THE WORK,
CATTE LAN SAID HIS WORK WAS MORE
AN ACT OF LOVE THAN A COMMENT
ON THE FINANCIAL WORLD.

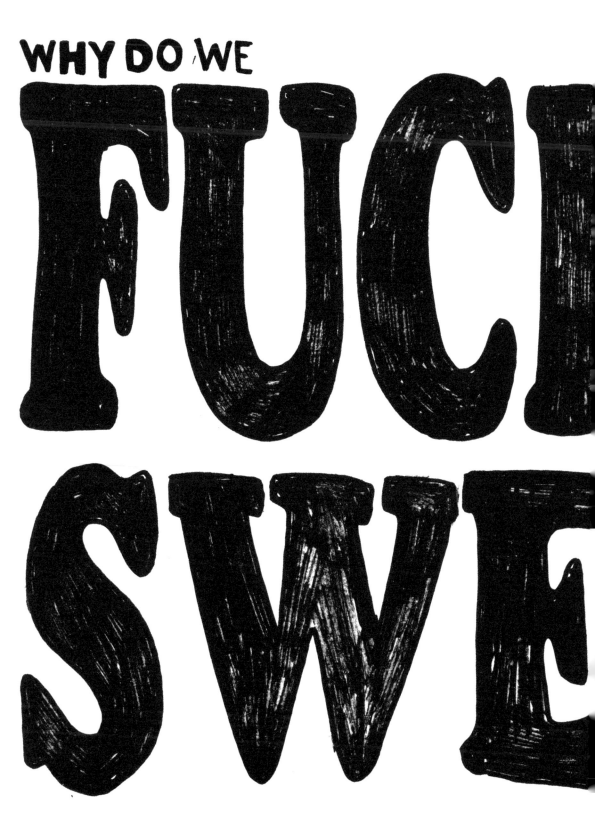

WHY DO WE
FUCI
SWE

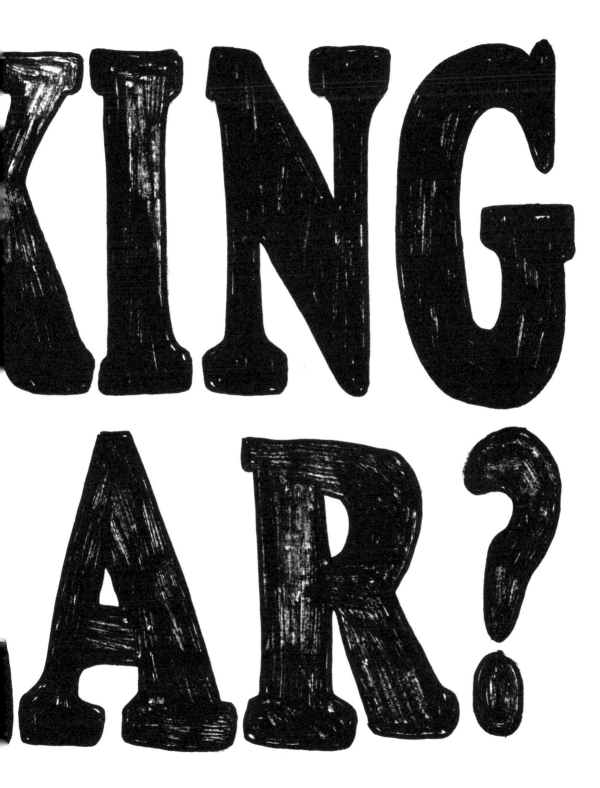

MALEDIC

TOLOGY

MA?

MALEDICTOLOGY (from Latin maledicere, "to say
something (dicere) BAD" and Greek "logia, study of)
is a branch of psychology, that does research
about swearing.
It is influenced by American psychologist TIMOTHY JAY
(Massachusetts College of Liberal Arts) and the
philologist and researcher in swearwords REINHOLD AMAN
(California). They assume that swearing & blustering
is part of the human life.
According to this, it can even act as a passiv self-defense
as it prevents palpable argument...

On̶ ̶t̶h̶e̶ ̶n̶e̶x̶t̶ ̶p̶a̶g̶e̶ Let's see what those boys have to say
on the following pages...

DR. TIMOTHY JAY

Professor in the PSYCHOLOGY department at MASSACHUSETTS COLLEGE OF LIBERAL ARTS.

swearing expert

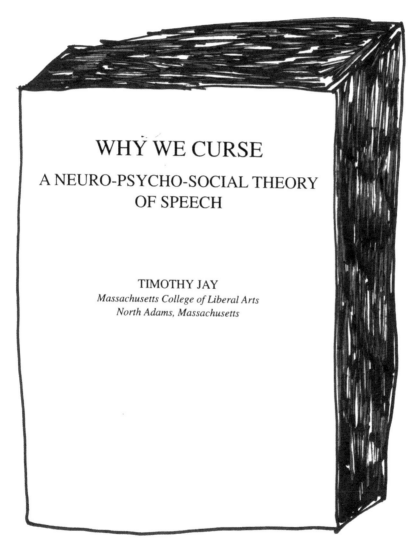

WHY WE CURSE

A NEURO-PSYCHO-SOCIAL THEORY OF SPEECH

TIMOTHY JAY

Massachusetts College of Liberal Arts
North Adams, Massachusetts

Dr. Timothy Jay is a professor in the
psychology department at Massachusetts
College of Liberal arts

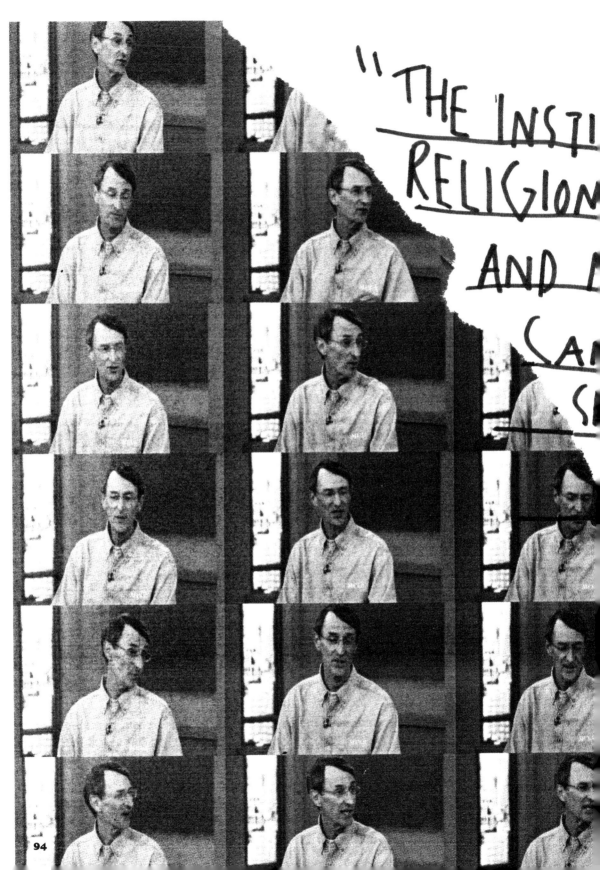

"THE INSTI
RELIGION
AND
CAN
SI

TIONS OF POWER;
THE COURTS, EDUCATION
DIA TELL US WHAT WE
SAY AND WHAT WE CANT
I DON'T THINK WE
VER REALLY HAD FREE
SPEECH IN THIS COUNTRY"

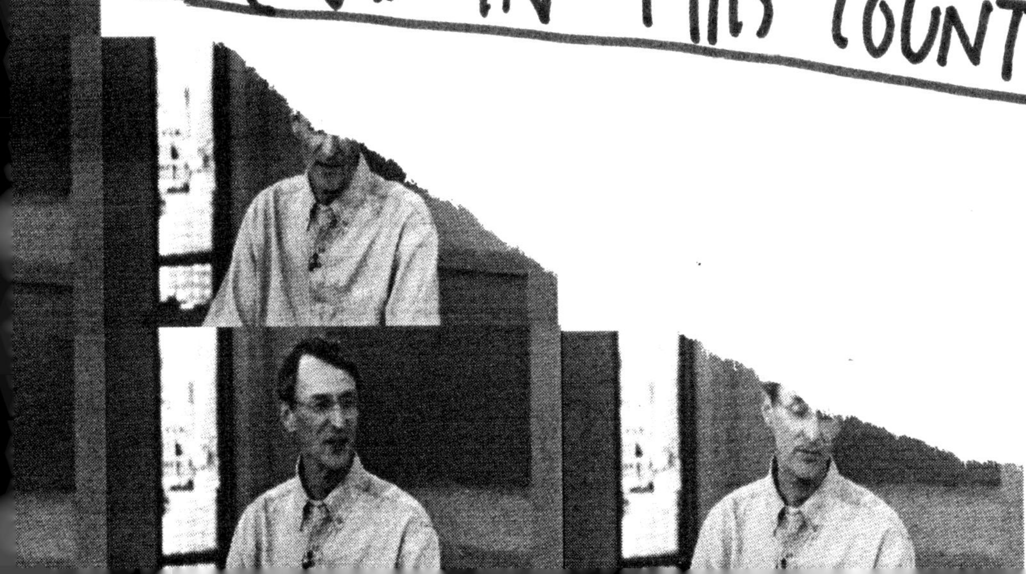

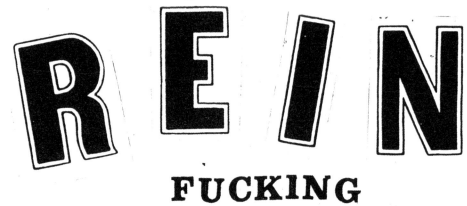

REINH

FUCKING

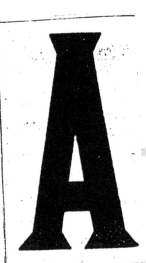

AMA

THE CUNNING

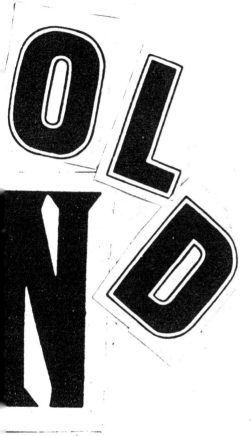

OLND

LINGUIST

"BAD WORDS" HAVE EXISTED
SINCE THE FIRST HUMANS
BUMPED THEIR TOES,
MISSED THEIR PREY OR
MET HOSTILE MEMBERS
OF ANOTHER PREHISTORIC TRIBE!

R. AMAN.

The man of swearing
The Noah Webster of verbal aggression.
Leading authority on abusive language.
When it comes to insults, he can hurl
them in 220 languages and, kind scholar
that he is, offer instant analysis of any
assaults' cultural significance.

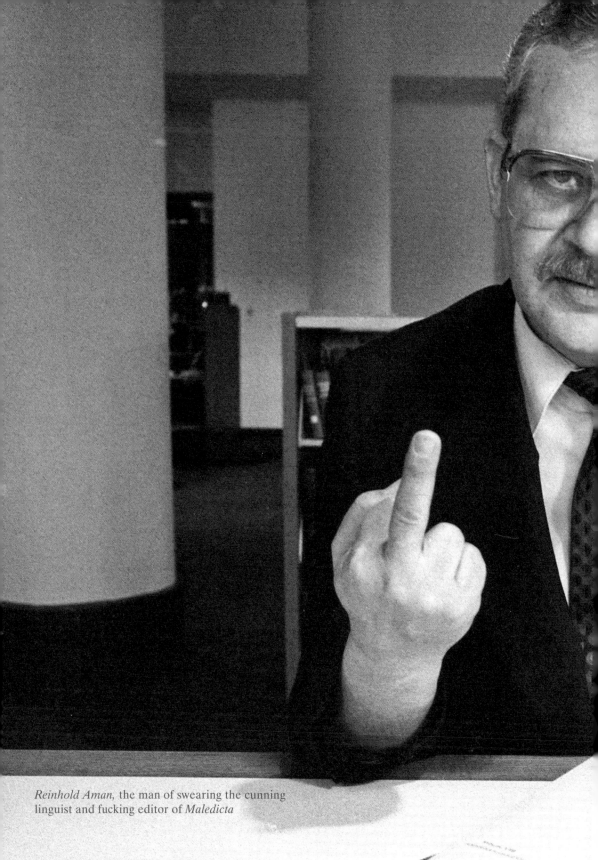

Reinhold Aman, the man of swearing the cunning
linguist and fucking editor of *Maledicta*

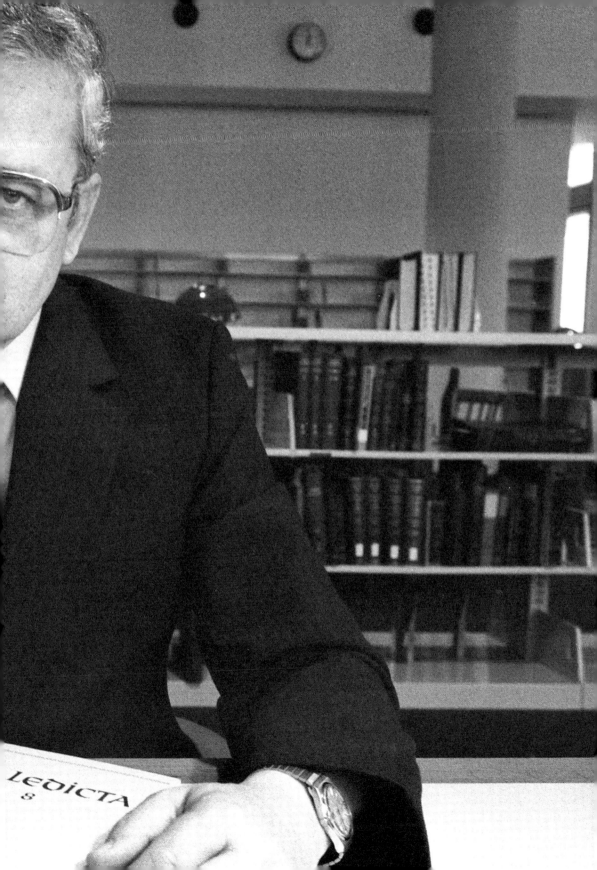

THE BEST OF

Maledicta

The International Journal of Verbal Aggression

A scholarly, scatological, and witty
investigation of outrageous insults,
forbidden language, and wicked jokes.

WARNING

Contains
Language
Offensive
to Blacks,
Catholics,
Gays, Jews,
Men, Women,
and WASPs.

"*Maledicta*'s ribald wit is so nicely matched with
scholarship that the journal is a real find."
—*Library Journal*

Edited by Reinhold Aman

"WITHOUT POWERFULL CURSE WORDS, HUMAN BEINGS WILL AGAIN BE THROWING STICKS AND STONES AND TRYING TO BREAK EACH OTHERS BONES."

Reinhold Aman, Maledicta Press, 1987:

Thus, 22 years ago, I decided to dedicate my life ~~for the~~ the collection and analysis of all those words and ~~expressions~~ expressions shunned by academia, and published the results in our annual journal, MALEDICTA, with the motto:

"THEY SAY IT) - WE PRINT IT."

This specialization has resulted ~~worldwide~~ in worldwide recognition and praise, but it has required me to develop a THICK SKIN AGAINST THE RIDICULE AND DAMNATION BY THE "cacademics" - those who look up to gynecologists,psychiatrists and other specialists in human illnesses, but who look down upon the few brave philologists who merely collect and study "dirty" words for "dirty" body parts.

To such people, the word is more repulsive than the thing for which it stands) a strange twist indeed but common in strait laced societies. Despite criticism, we will carry on, compelled by a childlike curiosity about human beings, while maintaining sensitivity to their feelings.

SWEARING AND THE BRAIN

SWEARING IS A SIGN OF HEALTHY BRAIN.

SWEARING HAS HIS ORIGIN IN THE
PART OF THE BRAIN, THAT ALSO HOSTES
EMOTIONS AND INSTINCTS: IT COMES FROM
OUR LIMBIC SYSTEM. THAT MEANS THAT
SWEARING IS INNATE AND HUMAN.
IT WOULD BE WRONG TO TRY TO STOP
SWEARING. SWEARING REDUCES PAIN
AND STRESS. SCIENTIST CONFIRMED THAT
IN SEVERAL EXPERIMENTS.
          NEGATIVE FEELINGS, LIKE ANGER
DISAPOINTMENT OR FEAR ORIGINATE IN
THE BRAIN WHEN A PERSON GETS STRESSED.
SWEARING DERIVES THESE FEELINGS
LIKE A LIGHTNING ROD ELECTRICITY.
SWEARING IS AN ANGER MANAGEMENT
TECHNIQUE, EXPERIMENTS IN THE PAST
SHOWED THAT SWEARING PUTS THE BODY
ON HIGH ALERT. IF THAT HAPPENS WE
FEEL LESS PAIN AND THE BODY GETS
READY TO EITHER FIGHT OR FLEE.
THIS AGAIN IS A SIMILARITY TO THE
FIRST HUMAN BEINGS. SWEARING IS
RELATED TO BASIC INSTINCTS.

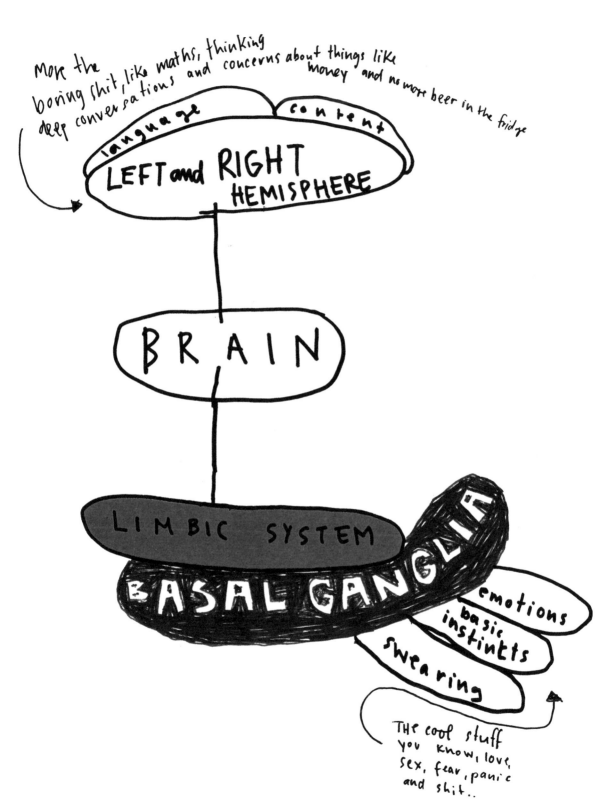

More the boring shit, like maths, thinking deep conversations and concerns about things like money and no more beer in the fridge

language   content

LEFT and RIGHT HEMISPHERE

BRAIN

LIMBIC SYSTEM

BASAL GANGLIA

emotions
basic instinkts
swearing

The cool stuff you know, love, sex, fear, panic and shit..

SWEARING IS A SIGN OF VERBAL INTELLIGENCE.

Thalamus

Putamen

Tail of caudate

Head of caudate

Globus pallidus

Amygdala

PEOPLE WHO SWEAR MORE HAVE STRONGER LANGUAGE SKILLS OVERALL.

We don't know everything about swearing in our brain but we do know that it comes from the limbic system and it's fucking good for you

SCIENCE

FUCKING

CONFIRMS

SWEARING

REDUCES

PHYSICAL AND MENTAL

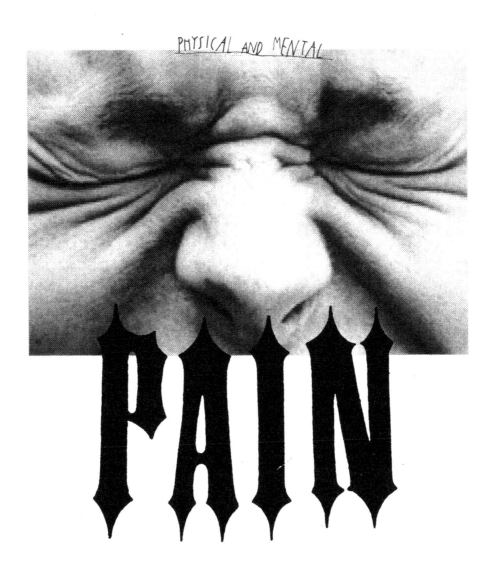

PAIN

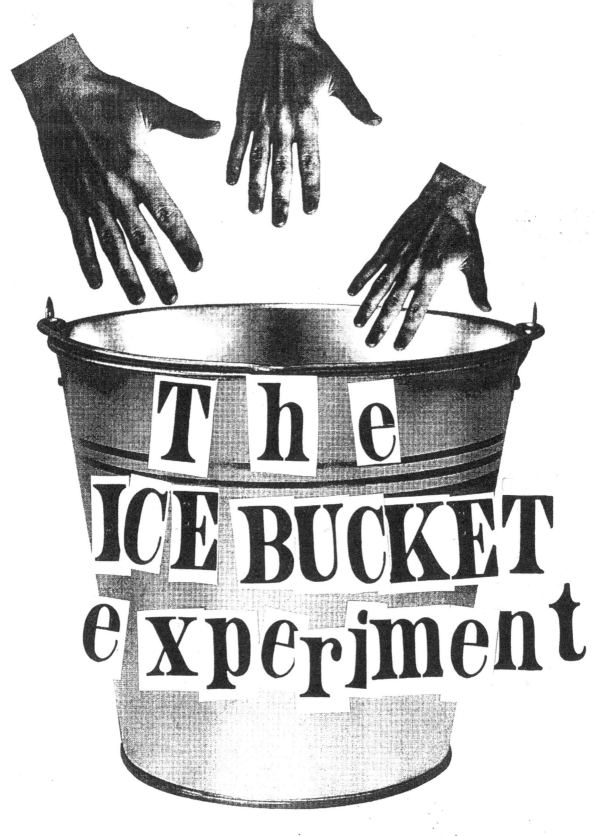

The ICE BUCKET experiment

Researchers from Keele University, Richard Stephens
John Attkins and Andrew Kingston published "Swearing
as a response to pain" in the magazine "neuro report",
finding out that some people could hold their hands in
ice water for twice as long as usual, if they swore, as
compared to if they used neutral words. They also reported
reported feeling less physical pain. They called this the ~~ICE~~
the ICE BUCKET EXPERIMENT.

STEPHENS THEREFORE SAYS:

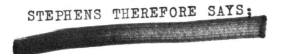

"I WOULD ADVISE PEOPLE TO SWEAR IF THEY HURT THEMSELVES!"

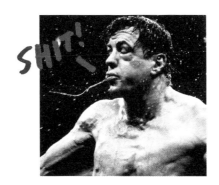

Now, let's take a moment
for a very speacial word...

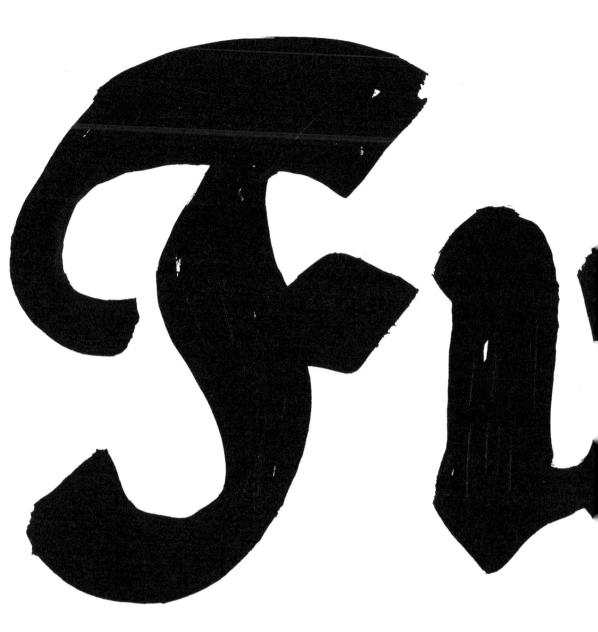

WHAT IS THE ETYMOLOGYCAL
ORIGIN OF THIS COPULATIVE WORD?

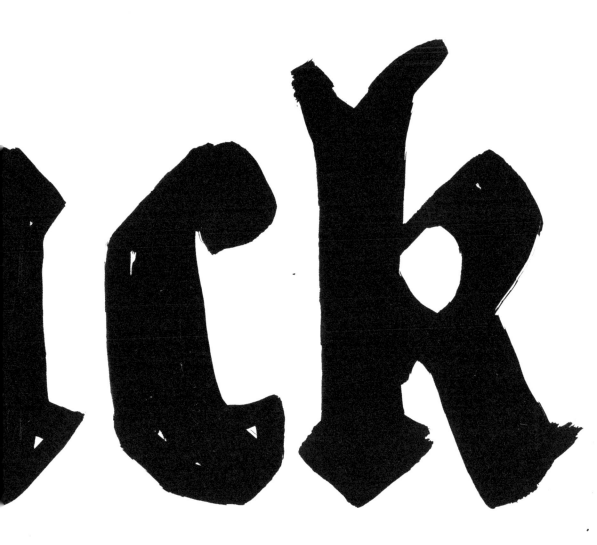

No one knows. It should not,however,constitute an insoluble
problem. No one seems to have been beguiled enough into
undertaking the necessary research. The Latin verb FUTUO,
 FUTUERE (tocopulate) may well be the ancestors on the standar
Standart English word, as may the German FICKEN (to strike,
hence,to copulate). The combination of German and Latin words,
the vocalism of the one with the consonantism of the other,
would yield F U C K. The Greek FITEUO and French FOUTRE, both
 meaning to have sexua l c onnection, almost certainlyhave
contributed to the ancestry of xxxxxxxxx the word.
 The verb and noun FUCK and the adjective FUCKING firstxx
 appear in print at the commencement of the sixteenth century
 in a poem published about I5o3 by the Scottish poet and
 onetime Franciscan friar WILLIAM DUNBAR.

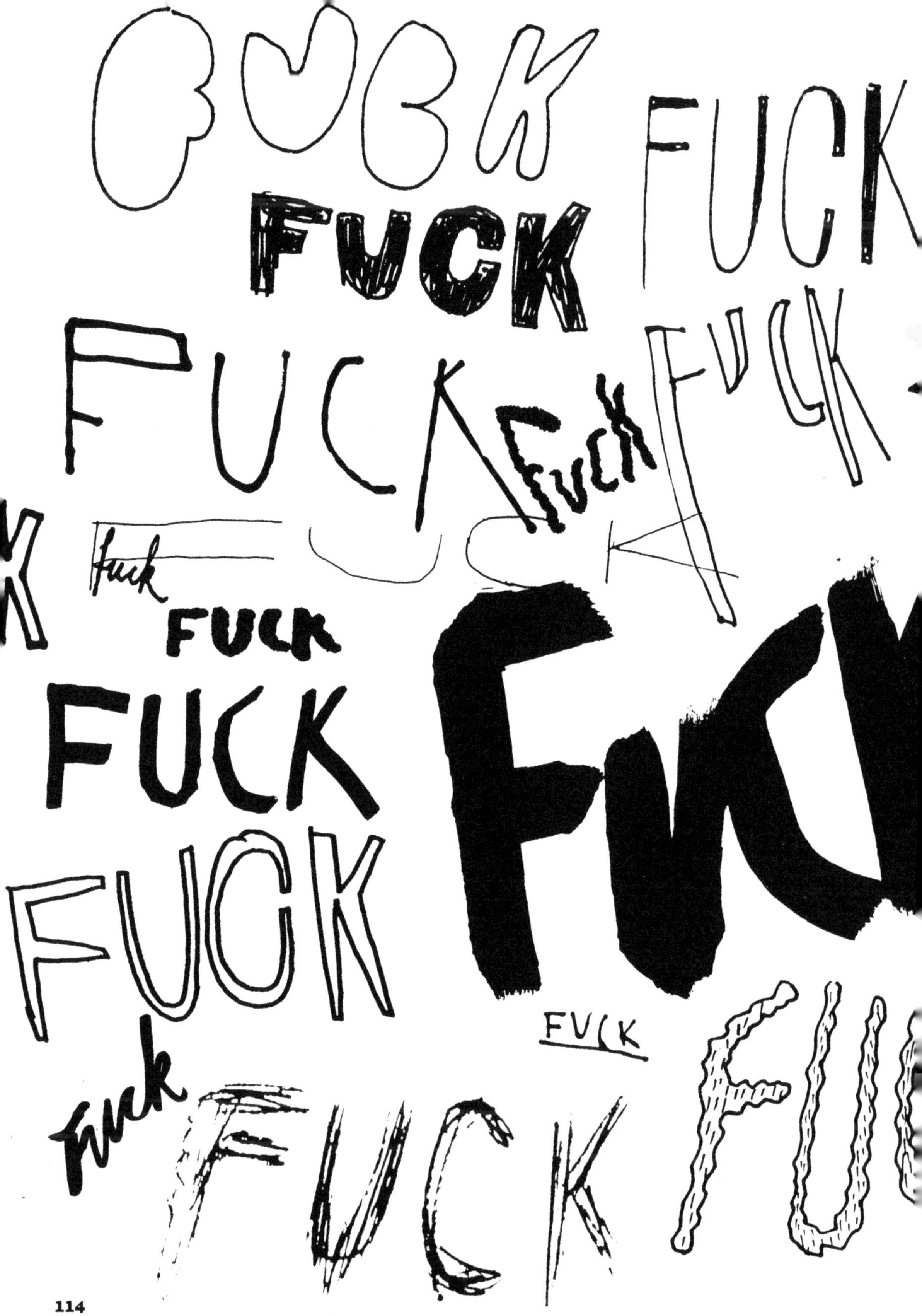

FUCK

FUCK

FUCK

FUCK

FUCK

FUCK

FUCK

K

Fuck

FUCK

FUCK

FUCK

FUCK

Fuck

FUCK

FUCK

FUCK

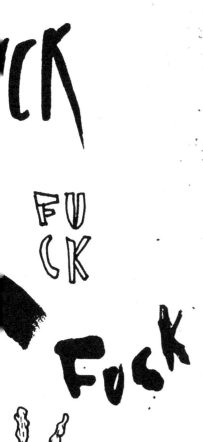

"Ane Brash of Wowing" ("A Bout of Wooing")
the last four lines of the poemread:

He clappit fast, he kist, and chukkit
As with the glaikis he wer ouiganes
Yit be his feirris he wald have fukkit;
Ye brek my hart, my bone ane!

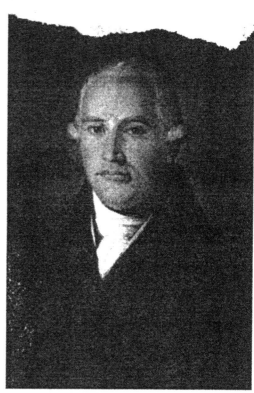

William Dunbar

Scottish poet, who was
perhaps the most important
poet of Scotland in the
early Renaissance.

First published *1503* in an scottish poem
by *William Dunbar* "FUCK" is today probably
the mostly used four letter word

115

THE
FORMS
OF
FUCK

With the exception of the mid-eighteen century fuck-beggar,
ah impotent man whom only a beggar woman would allow near her;
fuck-finger or finger-fucker, a female masturbator; and fuck fist,
a~~emilaymanvanb~~ator, the forms of FUCK are mostly nineteenth-twentieth
a male masturbator
century inven~~tho~~
century inventions.

FUCK (IT),
a low expletive, correctly described by Partridge as "Verygen. among
those for whom delicacy and aesthetics mean little-or rather nothing"

FUCK OFF,
get out, go, depart,make off.

FUCK YOU JACK, I'M ALL RIGHT;
a catchphrase directed at callousness or indifference,said to be
nautical origin, popular among military personnel in WORL D WAR I and
later abbreviated ~~tixftixxxiexfit~~ to "I'm all right Jack."

FUCKABLE,
sexually desirable,nubilem

FUCKED-UP AND FAR FROM HOMEX,
in the depths of misery, a British military catmhphrase, ca. I898

FUCKER,
chap, fellow,man, lover.

FUCKSOME,
sexualy desirable.

FUCK-PIG,
ah unpleasant man.

FUCK UP,
to make a mess of, as in Snafu, Situatmn normal, all fucked up.

FUCKISH
ready for copulation.

FUCKING,
an intensivem as adjective; the sexual act, as a noun.

FUCKSTER, FUCKSTRESS?
a notable performer or addict to them sexual act.

(to) GET FUCKED or TO GET A FUCKING,
to be cheated or be btrayed.

TO FUCK AROUND or TO FUCK THE DOG,
to waste time, loaf or idle.

TO FUCK ONE'S WAY OUT,
to cheat or defraud.

MILITARY USE

ARMY CREOLE WAS A TERM USED IN TOM WOLFE'S BOOK "THE RIGHT STUFF" TO DESCRIBE AN ENGLISH DIALECT SPOKEN BY MILITARY ~~PERSONAL~~ PERSONNEL. THIS DIALECT RELIES UPON EXTENSIVE USE OF PROFAN INTENSIFIERS LIKE **FUCK** TO GAIN ATTENTION IN CONFUSING CIRCUMSTANCES REQUIRING PROMPT, DECISIVE ACTION.

BEFORE 1980, BASIC TRAINING DRILL INSTRUCTORS USED THE DIALECT TO INCREASE THE STRESS-LEVELS OF RECRUITS. MILITARY PERSONNEL LEARNING THE DIALECT IN TRAINING MAY USE IT TO IMPROVE COMMUNICATION IN STRESSFUL SITUATIONS.

The word was used to induce stress during military recruit training
and became a dominant element of an English military dialect identified
by Tom Wolfe as ~~xxx armyxxxxk~~ Army Creoly
by Tom Wolfe as Army creole. A succinct example of the flexibility
of the word is its use almost every word in a sentence.

Extract from Wolfe's book "Wartime: Understanding and behaviour in
the Second World War

Once, on a misty a Scottish airfield, an airman was changing the magneto
on the engine of a Wellington bomber. Suddenly his wrench slipped and
he flung it on the grass and snarled:

"FUCK! THE
FUCKING FUCKER
IS FUCKED!"

The bystanders were all quite well aware that he had stripped a bolt
and skinned his knuckles.

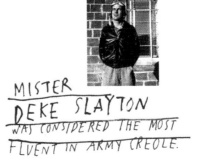

MISTER
DEKE SLAYTON
WAS CONSIDERED THE MOST
FLUENT IN ARMY CREOLE.

FALCONY CODES

MILITARY PILOTS WOULD USE CODED
CREOLE. THE CODED DIALECT WOULD
BE SPOKEN AS "FALCON" FOLLOWED BY
A NUMBER. FALCON-ONE-ZERO-FOUR, FOR
EXAMPLE, IS THE CODE FOR "WHAT THE FUCK? OVER"
AN EMPHATIC VERSION OF "SAY AGAIN. OVER")

```
0    - Fuck
00   - Shit hot
000  - If CAG saw that he'd shit
101  - You've got to be shitting me
102  - Get of my fucking back
103  - Beats the shit out of me
104  - What the fuck, over.
105  - It's so fucking bad I can't believe it
106  - I hate this fucking place
107  - This place sucks
108  - Fuck you very much
109  - That gd SOB
110  - Beautiful. Just fuckin beautiful
111  - Here comes another fucking CAG ops brainstorm
112  - Big fuckin Deal
113  - Let me talk to that son of a bitch
114  - Get your shit together
115  - You bet your sweet ass
116  - Fuck it.
117  - I love you so fucking much - I could shit.
118  - We eat this shit up
119  - Adios Motherfucker
120  - That's a no-no
121  - Fuck it, I got mine (FIIGMO)
124  - That god damn O club
126  - You piss me off
136  - If you ask for another low pass one more time, you
       will not get launched for a fucking week. over.
137  - You may not have any fucking fuel
138  - My fucking bladder hurts
139  - I have a motherfucking prostate overpressure light
140  - Comex motherfucker
142  - The fucking helos are all fucked again
143  - It's the air boss' fault
144  - Shut up and fly that fucking airplane
209  - While you were gone the whole world turned into shit
221  - Fuck you and the horse you rode in on
222  - You may not like the fucking CAG staff but the CAG staff
       likes fucking you.
223  - Get your head out of your ass
224  - You say "I don't Know" one more time  and I'm gonna
       shove a sonobouy up your ass
```

```
225  - You must have ak s shit for brains
226  - Would you like a kick in the ass to help you get your airborne
227  - What does it take to get a clearance out of this fucking place
228  - Just fly the iron bus and leave the ASW to us
229  - You're so fucking stupid you're a menace to society
230  - This bastard has more downing gripes than the USS Arizona
231  - Comments are recommendations my ass
232  - Just out of curiosity NAV, where the fuck are we?
233  -IIt's interval, as fas as I'm circumcised
269 -- Excuse me Sir, but you obviously have me confused with
        somebody who gives a shit

500  - Those fucking bl ack shoe motherfuckers
501  - Those fucking rear echelon motherfuckers
600  - Those fucking ASW pukes
641  - Hang it in your fucking ear
700  - Fucking grunts
728  - If I hear "CV" concept one more time I'm gonna puke
750  - That fucker runs like a well oiled machine
775  - Your old lady wears combat boots
800  - I love this so much I can't shit
901  - If it's such a good fucking deal send _____
902  - If I called for shit you'd come sliding in o a shovel
1000 - Cool in the Padre is here
3000 - Hay for the horses, whiskey for my men and a plate of flie s
        for my toad
3001 - He's so light, he's a menace to aviation
3002 - He just had his fucking tubes cut
3003 - He hasn't had hi  fucking lobotomy yet
3032 - Not so fucking fast
```

XXX

'FALCONY CODES' are coded army creole messages,
military pilots would use to communiate with each other

APPENDIX
further reading on the
world of swearing

Bibiliography & List of Sources

1.The Anatomy of Swearing by Ashley Montagu, 1967. **2.**UK Essays, https://www.ukessays.com/essays/communications/hand-gestures-history-and-usage-communications-essay.php, 2015. **3.**Wikipedia, https://en.wikipedia.org/wiki/The_finger, 2016.**4.**Tanscript "Filthy Words", http://law2.umkc.edu/faculty/projects/ftrials/conlaw/filthywords.html, 1972. **5.** The Science of Sweraing, Michelle Drews, https://harvardsciencereview.com/2014/01/23/the-science-of-swearing/. **6.**Why We Curse: A Neuro-psycho-social Theory of Speech e, Dr. Timothy Jay,2000. **7.** David Templeton, Rude Words: Santa Rosa professor is the 'Noah Webster of verbal aggression', Sonoma Independent, Feb. 15-21, 1996. **8.** Swearing as a response to pain, article in Neuroreport, Richard Stephens, John Atkins, Andrew Kingston, 2009

THE ANTIQUITY OF SWEARING

Extract of the book "The Anatomy of Swearing" by Ahley Montagu

How old is swearing? It is as old as man and coeval with language. How old is man? Very near two million or more years. And speech? One may estimate that it began at about the same time. Interestingly enough many philologists have held that speech originated in utterances closely akin to swearing. According to this theory,

spoken language began when a cry of pain, formerly wrung out by real suffering, and seen to be understood and sympathized with, was repeated in imitation, no longer as a mere instinctive utterance, but for the purpose of intmating to another, "I am (was, shall be) suffering"; when an angry growl, formerly the direct ecpression of passion, was reproduced to signify disapprobation and threatening, and the like. This was enough to serve as a foundation for all that should be built upon it.

This view, here expressed by *William Dwight Whitney*, who, in the 1890s, was professor of Sanskrit and Comparative Philology at Yale, has found many distinguished proponents. The development of this theory runs something like this: Before men developed any articulate means of communication with each other, there were already in existence certain emotinally highly charged sounds or explectives. These sounds had arisen in response to the need of relieving angry feelings or giving expression to one,s feelings upon a sudden shock or surprise. This need was fundamentally a phys-iological. Such expletive sounds were not invented by man but were physiologically determined for him by the shape of his chest and the form of his nasal cavities, throt, and larynx. Such sounds would occur, as it were, in spite of himself and only upon the experience of some sudden shock, whether of pain, annoyance, or surprise. The elementary and undeveloped forms of such sounds are universally the same among all men of all lands and times. For example, the fundamental tone of the human voive is *ah*, or *a*, voiced as in "father". This sound, as an exclamation, is found among all known peoples, as are its variant forms *oh*, *oo*, *ow*, *ugh*, *oi*, *eh* and so on. The elementary forms of there sounds are not acquired, nor are they inherited. They are physologically determined; that is to say, physiologically determined in the sense that a volume of air suddenly ecpelled through the throat will cause certain specific sounds to be produced quite involuntarily. Since such sounds are initiated in the throat, they are vowel sounds, for that is where vowels are pro-duced. For this reason the fundamental character of these expressions, no matter how obscured they may have become by the verlaying cultural style, remains unchanged wherever men speak. It is evident that these words are of such a nature that they are capable of conveying their meaning to men who are unacquainted with eachother's language, for it is the basic affective or emotional tone of the word that constitutes its meaning. Without their peculiar affective tones these phys-iological, or organic, words lose their meaning; for example, an expressionless *oh* or *ugh* means nothing, but given full organic value they assume significance. It is in this sense that Whitney wrote, at the beginning of the passage already quoted, "The tones significant of feeling, of which no one can deny the existence because they are still part of our expression, are fully capable of becoming the effective initiators of language."

While such a theory of language has its attrac-tions, it can at best be regarded only as an expla-nation of the origin of some words and of certain parts and processes of language. Discussions of the origin of language are by no means unrewarding, not so much for what they tell us of the origin of language as for what they tell us of its elementary forms. As *C.H. Grandgent* has remarked, "How language originated nobody knows and everybody has told." It is probable that most, if not all, theories of the origin of language have some substance, but alone or together they are at most capable only of suggesting how certain aspects of speech may have come into being. The "bow-wow" theory holds that primitive words originated in the imitation of the sounds of animals, principally the barking of dogs. The "pooh-pooh" theory holds that language is derived from instinctive ejaculations called forth by pain or other intense feelings or sensations. The "ding-dong" theory claims that there is a peculiar harmony between sound and sense, that each thing has its peculiar ring, and that this was vocally imitated by primitive man. The "yo-he-ho" theory suggests that speech originated in the breathing relief associated with intense muscular effort. More than one author has suggested that at least one of the most prominent uses of language is to dissipate superfluous and obstructive nerve force — in plain English, to reduce nervous tension. The "gestural" theory holds that speech came into being when men began to imitate with their tongues the gestures they made with their bodies. The theory that goes by the charming name of "tarara- boom-de-ay" has it that speech originated in the collective half- musical expressions of early man when his principal vocal exercise was a meaningless humming or singing.

Suppose that a group of such early men have together succeeded in bringing down a great mammoth; they will at once spontaneously be filled with joy and will strike up a chant of triumph — say, something like "tarara-boom-de-ay." The sounds of the chant might easily come to mean "We have brought him down. We have conquered. Hooray! Let us give thanks." And so on from there. This theory has been suggested by Otto Jesperson, and it is remarkably true that what can- not be uttered can often be sung. Finally, there is the "tally-ho" theory, suggested by myself, that speech came into being as a result of the necessities of communication arising during the cooperative hunting of early man. What we learn from examining the various theories of speech is that most writers on the subject agree that it is highly probable that some of the earliest elements of speech were initiated by the desire to express oneself forcefully. Swearing, therefore, is probably coeval with the birth of language; however, it cannot be regarded as the sole or even the principal

stimulus to the origin of speech, but at most as a contributory or dynamic factor in its development. Something of the manner of the use of words among early men may be inferred from the studies that have been made on the languages of living nonliterate peoples. Such studies are important for the proper understanding of the role that words play in swearing.

The Use and Meaning of Words in the Languages of Nonliterate People:

The study of the languages of nonliterate peoples has revealed the fact that words play the part essentially of *implements* Words are regarded as capable of *doing* things, not however in themselves or when they are isolated, but when they are properly handled In examining the structure of a "primitive" language we are at once impressed by the *operative* function that the words seem to possess, Malinowski writes of the language of the Trobriand Islanders:

A word means to a native the proper use of the thing for which it stands, exactly as an implement means something when it can be handled, Simi- larly a verb, 3 word for an action, receives its meaning through an active participation in this action. A word is used when it can produce an action and not describe one, still less to translate thoughts, The word therefore has a power of its own, it is a means of bringing things about, it is a handle to acts and objects and not a definition of them ... Language in its primitive function is to be regarded as a mode of action rather than as a countersign of thought.

Significantly enough, it is the *affective* value, the feeling tone, of the word that is bound up with its meaning; the *affective* value is also the sense of active participation in the action for which the word stands. This active participation (in the action for which the word stands) need not be overt, but may be, and indeed most usually is, only felt. The word "empathy," or feeling into, best expresses this participative character of the word complex. If we may anticipate a little here, it may he pointed out that in the process of swearing, the words employed are generally of notably high afiective value and are preeminently used as implements where- with to belabor their object. This was, for example, explicitly recog- nized in the behavior of certain Arabs who, when cursed, ducked their heads or fell flat on the ground in order to avoid a direct hit. I have also seen this very fully recognized in Union Square in New York by a young man who was for some reason being most proficiently sworn at by a slightly intoxicated Irishman. At every curse the young man pretended to wince, as if each oath was a stick upon his back, and to put a finishing touch to the performance, he raised an arm and ducked his head behind it, as if to ward off every verbal whack delivered by the irate derelict.

Among certain tribes of Australian aborigines when a man wishes to bespatter another he swears at him, but should he find that this words have been overheard by one who stands in a certain social relation to him, he will exclaim, "My mouth is foul." On such an occasion the individual will sometimes take a lighted firebrand and pass it backward and forward before his mouth in ritual purification. The dynamic quality of such words is well illustrated here. Whether the words are in reality invested with a tangible power or not is of no consequene here, for the fact is that they are regarded as possesing befouling qualities, precisely as if they possessed them in some substantial physical form. Hers the function of words in their affective aspect and as a mode of action is given proper emphasis. We must remember this "primitive" character of words and language.

Swearing among nonliterate people

The term "primitive" as applied to many nonliterate peoples is a misnomer, since the cultures of such peoples are in many ways no less complex than our own; hence, anthropologists prefer to use the term "nonliterate peoples," although that is not altogether satisfactory either. But it is the preferred term, and we shall continue to use it here when referring to those cultures and peoples that, at the time they were described, had not yet been seriously influenced by the more "advanced" cultures.
The information relating to swearing among nonliterate peoples is very limited. Ethnologists apparently have not considered the subject worthy their attention. Interestingly enough, the only reports on the swearing of nonliterate peoples that we possess come from two Australian ethnologists and refer to widely separated Australian aboriginal tribes. The white Australian, as we shall later have occasion to see, numbers among his fellows perhaps the most inveterate and unimaginative swearers that exist anywhere in the world today. May it not be that the interest of Dr. Her-

bert Basedow and Donald F. Thomson in the swearing of the aboriginesvowes something to this fact? However this may be, the culture of the Australian aborigines is generally held to be at a Stone Age level of technological development. It is, therefore, fortunate that such reports of the swearing of nonliterate peoples as we do have should relate largely to these aborigines. Basedow writes, of Australian tribes in general, "A common disturbance of the peace is brought on by petty theft. One woman might, intentionally or otherwise, appropriate a small article belonging to another. When the article is missed by the owner, an argument ensues, which soon warms up to a strained pitch of excitement. Abusive epithets become prolific, which repeatedly embody references to excrement and other filth".

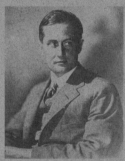

Donald Fergusson Thomson, (*26 June 1901 – †12 May 1970) was an Australian anthropologist and ornithologist who was largely responsible for turning the Caledon Bay crisis into a "decisive moment in the history of Aboriginal-European relations". He is remembered as a friend of the Yolngu people, and as a champion of understanding, by non-Indigenous Australians, of the culture and society of Indigenous Australians

We shall see from the next report, by Thomson, relating to the swearing of a number of tribes inhabiting the Cape York Peninsula, that references to excrement and other filth is also a common form of swearing among these relatively isolated peoples.
Thomson states that among the tribes investigated by him there was no general prohibition upon reference to the genitalia or the physiological functions of reproduction, defecation, and urination. Children grow up with no inhibitions in these matters except in the presence of certain relatives toward whom it is obligatory to exercise restraint. Children learn to swear at a very early age, as Thomson discovered when "In a camp of the Yintjingga tribe on the estuary of the Stewart River, a child about two years of age that was being suckled at its mother's breast, dropped the nipple to glower at me and exclaim in the Ompela language of its mother, 'Awu! kuna katta! kuna kata!' 'Devil! excrement foul! excrement foul!'" Thomson tells us that nobody expressed concern or at» tempted to correct the child, whereas among other tribes he found that this would have been done at once.

As among ourselves, so among these tribes, "there are at least two, often a number, of words for each object, or for parts of the body. One of these words is generally considered to be the proper term to be used in ordinary polite conversation; the other is, in the words of my aboriginal informant, 'half swear.'" In the use of these words, Thomson noted, a very definite etiquette is rigorously observed, and as he points out, the aborigines are here characterized "by a nice reserve and by a sense of 'good taste' that we are always apt to claim as our special prerogative."We begin to perceive that the swearing of the Australian aborigines assumes a most startling family likeness to our own. But before proceeding with its further examination, let us continue a little with our account of the forms of swearing among these Cape York tribes. When our aboriginal . . . inadvertently strikes his toe against a stump or root he does not break out with an oath or obscene expression, but calls upon the name of a relative long deceased. Similarly, when a weapon upon which he is working, or a canoe lashing, breaks, he calls upon the name of a dead realation whose name has outlived the kintja (tabu) period following death...

This practice of calling upon the name of a deceased relation, a mild and innocuous oath, is general among the native tribes of Cape York Peninsula, and is found in tribes in widely separated localities.Thomson writes that "in three years spent among these natives I never knew them to depart from their traditional behavior and to use foul or obscene expressions under stress of pain, fear, or surprise, although these are freely used under other circumstances." He classifies the swearing employed by these tribes as consisting of two main types:

1.Unorganized swearing and obscenity, falling under no sanction and used by both sexes in quarrels, and as taunts to goad an enemy to fight. This type of swearing is known to the Wik Monkan people as kulken-tanak, "anger make-for,""i.e., "for the purpose of arousing anger," for which purpose it is deliberately employed Under this category fall all the worst expressions in the language: deadly insults that it would be intolerable for any native to receive in public

2. Organized or licensed swearing and swearing that is not only permissible, but obligatory, between those who stand in certain relationships under the clas-sificatory system, It is carried out in public, and falls under a definite social sanction. This organized license is in direct contrast with the extreme tabu (kintja) of certain relationships, eg., with the wife's mother, the wife's father, and the wife's brothers. It is supposed to induce a state of euphoria: in the words of my informants, to "make everybody happy? This falls again into two distinct types:

a) Obscenity pure and simple, consisting of more or less stereotyped references to the pudenda, and permitted between a very few relatives, frequently in the grandparentgrandchild generations, and almost always between persons of the same sex. Certain relatives are also per- mitted to snatch playfully at one another's genitalia, and even to handle the organs in public.

b). Bad language, consisting chiefly of references to the anus and to excrement, permissible or obligatory between a number of relatives, generally distant, with whom license of a restricted type is permitted The use of Obscenities, or any sexual behavior is prohibited.

From Thomson's account it is evident that swearing frequently occurs among these tribes. Furthermore, there is also prevalent a special kind of swearing which is restricted to individuals who stand in a certain relationship to one another. The interesting thing about this custom is that it is not only socially sanctioned but obligatory on the part of the persons concerned. This type of behavior is known to ethnologists as the joking relationship, after the similar form of behavior first recorded for several Indian tribes of North America.

Without entering into a detailed discussion of the character of these joking relationships, it may briefly be said here that they are intimately associated with the kinship organization of the tribe and the relationship in which every individual is classified in, relation to every other member of the tribe For example, under the restraints of ordinary social life the strictest prohibitions govern the relations of oneself to one's wife's mother, the wife's father, and the wife's brothers. To balance these prohibitions the greatest freedom is permitted with a member of one's classificatory grandparental generation, Between the members of these generations organized obscenity and behavior of a playful sexual type, such as snatching at one another's genitalia — always in the presence of the other members of the tribe, whether of the prohibited degrees or not — is the normal form of behaviori As a rule restraint must be exercised with all one's blood relations, while the more distant in the classificatory system are the individuals, the greater is the freedom permitted in the joking relationship. But the greatest free dom is permitted between the grandparent and grandchild generations, or the *pola* (father's father) and his classificatory son's son, the *paladu*.

At the time when the sacred initiations take place at the sacred grounds and the men get together in a kind of temporary men's club, they exchange all sorts of ObscenitiWes and insults with each other, exchanges that in other cireimistances would be intolerable During all this the greatest good humor is maintained and much mirth is generated, When asked why they swear, the men actually reply, "Nothing, friend, make happy little but, no swear proper!"

If it is not already obvious, Thomson gives us the clue to the meaning of this kind of behavior. He writes: „There is no doubt that the exchanges under the joking relationship do provoke genuine mirth, as well as a ritual state of well-being, that counterbalances, relieves, and gives point to, the austerity and restraint that characterize much of the behavior under the kinship system.

Will not the gentle reader pause awhile with me and reflect in admiration upon the remarkably humane and intelligent manner in which these so-called primitive peoples have handled a problem that the selfstyled civilized peoples of the West have failed both to understand and to control, and have therefore condemned out of hand? Instead of condemning obscenity and swearing, the Australian aborigines have obviously made an endeavor to understand them. In this they have succeeded eminently well, and they have so utilized these forms of behavior as to make them serve extremely important and useful functions: as relief mechanisms for feelings that might otherwise be more dangerously expressed and as counter balances, also of relief and well-being, to the rigors, austerity, and restraints of much of social life. It is, indeed, not for nothing that all who have come to know the Australian aboriginal well have remarked upon the beauty of his character and the fact that he is a remarkably happy and well-integrated person.Socialized, or organized, swearing is the Australian aborigine's method of providing for the socially sanctioned expression of these forms

of conduct that are prohibited under other circumstances. It is the licitly provided escape valve that in a far cruder form finds expression in our own society at stag parties and in dirty jokes, obscene limericks, and the like, where forbidden matters are discussed that, as Benvenuto Cellini would have put it, are to be mentioned only under the apothecary's counter.

This form of socialized swearing (which is also to be found among Eskimos) constitutes one of the most Widely diffused and efficient devices for assisting to preserve the equilibrium of the individual and his society. But let us continue. In all the tribes investigated by Thomson, humorous and ribald remarks relating to various parts of the body are used in a jocular fashion, and most of these remarks are regarded as perfectly harmless unless they are addressed to a person who stands in a forbidden relationship. Here are some of the words that are so used among the Wik Monkan tribe of the Cape York Peninsula.

Extending all the way from merely jocular references to the hands, face, and legs to obscene references to the pudenda, they constitute the grossest insults possible in the language:

meritti	big eye
yanantti	plenty hair
koknn werra	wide ears
yank onk	long legs
ka onk	long nose
ma,a punkta wakk	arm like grass
tump many	little legs, thin legs
kutjaketti	big head
kutajak onk	long head

These terms are obviously blood-brothers to our "rubber neck", "baldy locks", "flap ears", "spindle legs", and the like. While such terms are, on the whole, quite innocent, they may be converted for use in dead earnest, as when a woman may say to a man who is looking at her, "Merriti!" "Big eye," that is to say, "what are you staring at you?". When a strong or offensive term is used playfully, the word puk (child or baby) is sometimes prefixed. "When used to an adult it has the force of a diminutive, a term of affection that takes the sting from the word accompanies. Thus, waiya, ‚bad', ‚a bad one'; puk waiya, in its literal sense ‚a bad child', is much the same as you little devil'."

Examples of more serious swering in the Wik Monkan language are the following:

To a man:

po,o wantji wenta	vagina woman mad
kuntjtut	big penis
kuntj tantitti	fat penis
kuntj mankatti	big penis root
untitti	big scrotum
otjumti	plenty urine

To a woman:

pam wenta	man crazy
po,o patj	bald pubis
po,o ka onk	vagina nose
po,o kati	enlarged clitoris
po,o tantitti	fatty vagina
po,o konnitti	big eared vagina

None of there terms, with the exception of one or two referring to the male pudenda that may be used in one of the joking relationships, is used joculary; all are employed only in the serious quarreling that is the prelude to fighting and are spoken in sharp tone of voice. They are expressions that are used when all restraint in cast aside.

Examining the forms of swearing employed among these Australian aborigines and the words utilized, we see that, with the exception of organ-ized swearing, these are of the same nature as our own. References to excrement and filth doubtless draw their sting for the purposes of swearing from the subjects' obnoxious qualities, which, as it were, may be hurled or spattered upon the objects of one's dislike. In order to be useful for the purposes of swearing, a word apparently must have reference to an object possessing, or thought to possess, force or power of some kind. Swearing is the process by means of which one seeks to use the power of something to chastise the object of one's swearing. The power of the thing is always intended to overcome the victim, is always to his disadvan-tage. The power may be a good, evil, or indifferent one. Thus, one may call upon the sun, commonly regarded as a powerful good, to burn up a neigh-bor's field – or his face. Or we may call our enemy a turdface. Here the turd is evil, evil-smelling, and evil looking powerfully so. Or we may liken his head to a block of wood, a rattle, or a bone in themselves neither good nor evil things, but pow-erfully hard or shallowly noisyi The value of terms referring to excrement and filth for the purposes

of swearing is fully recognized by the Australian aborigines, and were we in possession of the necessary information concerning other peoples elsewhere in the world we would doubtless find that this has been equally recognized by most or all of them. There is good reason to believe that the employment of such terms in swearing is very widely distributed if not universal.

Thomson's account of the native child of about two years who dropped his mother's breast to glower and swear at him, "Devil! excrement foul, excrement foul!" is interesting, as well as amusing. It is probable that the child was more than two years old, for white observers almost invariably underestimate the age of native children.

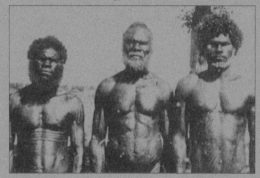

It is quite a common thing for a three or four year old native child to be suckled by his mother: But the important point is not the child's age or even that he swore, but the words he used and the reason for his swearing. The words give us the clue to the reason. The child's reaction, indeed, is a completely human and universal one.

Observing a white man, a strange creature at best, the child could no longer in comfort proceed with its meal. Frustrated and perhaps a little frightened by this unusual creature, the white man, the child called him a name equivalent to our word "devil," referring, doubtless, to his presumed unearthly origin, and swore at him in order to beat him off. The universality of this sort of response is well illustrated by the story told of a Devon yokel who on seeing a stranger walking down the road in his own direction remarked to his crony, "Aye, William, there be un stranger comen, Let's heave un brick at un." What the little Stewart River aboriginal simply was doing was "heaving a brick" at the stranger, and he did this with the only implement at his command, swearing. Among the Australian aborigines the name of a long deceased relative is often uttered as an exclamation upon the experience of a sudden shock, such as stubbing one's toe against the root of a tree, or when something upon which one is working suddenly breaks. This may at first appear to have no counterpart among ourselves. But, as we shall see, this is not strictly so.

In order to understand why the Australian calls upon the name of some long-deceased relative to serve him as an exclamation, it is necessary to know something of the religious beliefs of these people. We need not here concern ourselves with the details, since for our purposes it will be enough to know that the Australian aboriginal believes that when a person dies his soul either returns to the place from which it came or goes away to some distant region in which to dwell. The names of the dead are for a long period after their death considered sacred and must not be pronounced by any of their living relatives. Hence a great constellation of inhibited emotions is built up about the names of such deceased relatives. During the period in which these names are under a taboo, their owners are capable of working much mischief unless they are properly respected. Hence, the degree of awe in which their names are held is very high. It will then no longer be difficult to understand why an Australian aboriginal invokes the name of a long-deceased ancestor when he seeks quick release for a sud» denly induced emotion. What is more natural than to exclaim by that very name whose use has for so long been prohibited? It is an innocent-enough exclamation now, but one that formerly would have brought dire consequences to the unsanctioned user.

To these natives such names serve precisely the same function as do the names of the gods, the saints, and the holy ones (from whom something of the taboos that had surrounded them have departed) for the civilized swearer of our own day. Had the Australians possessed saints and gods, they would have sworn by them, and had we been forbidden to mention the names of our departed relatives for a long time after their decease, we, too, would have sworn, or at least exclaimed, by them. Indeed, in civilized societies some people do swear by one or other or both of their departed parents.

Again, we may observe that there is here no essential difference between the form of swearing used by the Australian aborigines and that which characterizes civilized men under similar conditions. The only difference is that the Australian aborigines exhibit a marked restraint in the form of the exclamations that they use under conditions in which civilized' men would employ foul and obscene expressions. Under the conditions of pain, fear, or surprise these natives indulge in none but the most innocent of exclamations, Such exclamations, however innocuous they may he, nonetheless constitute swearing, in much the same sense that it is swearing to utter the words "Holy Moses!" "Ye Gods!" or "Saint Patrick!"

It is of great interest to learn that under the conditions of a minor shock or surprise the aboriginal utters an exclamation that is the exact equivalent of the English "Oh, mother!" Here, as among ourselves, of course, the exclamation derives its power from the strong emotional attachment that exists between mother and child.

Swearing during quarrels, swearing as taunts to goad an enemy to fight, and swearing with obscene references to the pudenda are all familiar forms to us. During quarrels and in the taunts calculated to produce a fight, the most obscene and intolerable insults are used, such as "Go and have intercourse with your mother." This is an insult that no man will brook. Among these aborigines, as among Western peoples where the same oath occurs, incest is considered one of the Worst crimes a man can commit. The great affective weight of such an oath is obvious. Similarly, oaths making reference to the pudenda or sexual organs draw their power and eltectiveness from the great value placed upon these organs and the emotional investment that is made in them, Hence, any refer- ence to another's organs as not being as they should be is both mortifying and shocking.

It is evident, then, that as far as the basic forms of swearing are concerned, the Australian aborigines, of Cape York at least, have developed all the forms that the so called culturally more advanced peoples have. If we possessed a roughly complete account of their swearing practices, we should no doubt find that they indulged in still other forms of swearing akin to our own. In one respect they have developed far beyond any of the peoples of Western cultures: their sanctioning of swearing under the appropriate conditions. Here, with far greater insight and understanding of such matters than civilized societies have achieved, swearing has been recognized as a function of the human psyche of great power for good as well as evil. Australian aboriginal society has taken this power and utilized it for good, "to make everybody happy," as the natives themselves say. It is a sort of ritualized letting oil of steam the induction of a general feeling of well being as a consequence of being permitted to enjoy to the full the freedom of what, under other conditions, is prohibited and would be considered the most heinous offense. By contrast with our undiscriminating condemnation of swearing, these Australian aborigines have shown themselves far more intelligent than we of the Western world, who have neither recognized the nature and meaning of swearing, nor perceived how to utilize it for good.

Because in many ways the culture of the Australian aborigines is said to be the most primitive existing at the present time, it would hardly be justifiable to conclude that the forms of swearing that they now practice are akin to those practiced by the earliest men. But what we may say, with some degree of security, is that the swearing of the Australian aborigines suggests that the tendency to strong expression through speech testifies to the basic similarity of human nature among all peoples everywhere, whether they swear or not.

The Author

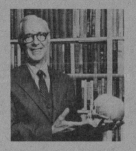

Montague Francis Ashley-Montagu (*June 28, 1905 – †November 26, 1999), previously known as Israel Ehrenberg, was a British-American anthropologist who popularized the study of topics such as race and gender and their relation to politics and development. He was the rapporteur in 1950, for the UNESCO statement The Race Question. As a young man he changed his name from Ehrenberg to „Montague Francis Ashley-Montagu". After relocating to the United States he used the name „Ashley Montagu". Montagu, who became a naturalized American citizen in 1940, taught and lectured at Harvard, Princeton, Rutgers, the University of California, and New York University. He authored over sixty books throughout this lifetime. In 1995, the American Humanist Association named him the Humanist of the Year.

"Swearing has been recognized as a function of the human psyche of great power for good as well as evil. Australian aboriginal society has taken this power and utilized it for good, to make everybody happy"

HAND GESTURES; HISTORY AND USAGE

Essay about the part of nonverbal communication called gestures

We are talking about the part of nonverbal communication called gestures. A gesture is a movement of the body or a part of it that is expressive of thought or feeling. However there is a degree of voluntarism. If someone pinches you and you flinch that is not a gesture. Gestures are a common part of communication that we all use to communicate everyday and most of us do not even think twice about using them. As gestures can include a wide range of things a narrower focus is required. For this paper I will be focusing on gestures specifically involving the use of hands and or fingers. First I will talk about research done on gestures. Second I will talk about the interaction between gestures and verbal language.

Let us first consider primates such as apes and chimpanzees. Primates are mostly visual animals. Just as in humans, for primates vision is more highly developed than any of the other four senses including the sense of sound. Consider for a moment what this might mean. Primates, with the exception of humans, have much better cortical control over hand movements than over voice, which is mostly restricted to emotionally based sounds controlled by sub cortical structures. This means that early hominids would have been better at expressive, voluntary communication using hands. Perhaps this explains why it is much easier to teach higher level primates sign language than it is to teach them to speak. One early study showed that a chimpanzee raised by humans could learn to speak only three or four words but gorillas and chimpanzees have learned several hundred manual signs.

However primates other than humans are restricted in using hands for communications because the arms and hands are also involved in postural support and locomotion. Most primates are adapted for living above ground in the tress. Apes live on the ground but move in a four legged fashion. Our closest genetic relatives, chimpanzees and gorillas, use what is known as knuckle walking in which the upper body is supported by the knuckles. Hominids are bipedal, walking upright which leaves their hands and arms free. There is speculation that the split that resulted in some great apes becoming hominids may have been caused by the formation of the Great Rift Valley in Africa. Those apes which were to become hominids were largely confined to the east of the valley. The discovery of a 3.5 million year old fossil in Chad which is west of the valley has caused some argument. However all other hominid fossils from between four million and two million years ago have been found to the east of the Great Rift Valley. Here the forests gave way to open grasslands called savannas. This new environment would have provided unique challenges for early hominids. They would have been vulnerable to specialized hunters and killers, the ancestors of tigers, lions, and hyenas. In this environment communication using gestures would have been much more effective than vocal communication. It is silent so predators are not alerted. It is also fundamentally spatial, and most of the information would have been spatial, such as locations of predators, easy prey, or food.

The earliest language being gestural would help explain how words came to be abstract rather than iconic. A leading figure in gesture research is psychologist Susan GoldinMeadow who has done several studies about the role of gestures in learning. It is a well established fact that students learn better if both words and hand gestures are used. Consider for example a teacher trying to illustrate water being poured into two containers of equal volume but different heights. The teacher will place one hand on top of the other and move them to illustrate differences in height. We do not always gesture when we speak. Also the type of gesture, the role in relation to what is being said, and the role in relation to the situation vary. If you wanted a person to stay away you would not use a gesture telling them to come closer. Someone of the other gender gesturing for you to come closer has different meaning then if it is done by a friend or parent. If you are talking about a fish you caught you will hold your hands apart horizontally versus if you are describing how big a baby has gotten your hand would be vertical.

Just like language gestures are not uniform to a culture or country. In the United States you wave your hand to say hello and goodbye. If you were in northern Europe you would wag your hand at the wrist. In Greece and Italy your palm would face inward and your fingers would be curled in. In Japan you bow slightly. How long and how deep you bow depends on the person. Let's go back to my earlier example of a gesture that means to come here. Here we curl one finger, usually the index, or all four fingers towards us. In the Philippines do not use the index finger. It is only used for dogs. In Latin America the index finger is a come on. In Indonesia and Australia it's used for prostitutes. In southern Europe using all your fingers would be saying goodbye. In Korea you would hold your arm out and move your fingers up and down. If someone puts their hand out in front with the fingers outspread here it means stop. In Lebanon it means no. If you were in Greece it's a curse. In Spain, Nigeria, and Chile it also has rude meanings. In the United States you typically point with your index finger to someone or something. In Europe pointing is not considered polite. In Africa you only point the index finger at inanimate objects. In China and Japan pointing is very rude. In Indonesia pointing with your index finger is very rude but you can use your thumb. In Zambia it is all right to point to objects. And In France if you do point it is best to do it discretely.

Some gestures are country specific. In the Netherlands grabbing a nonexistent fly in front of your face is saying someone is nuts. In Poland flicking a finger against someone's neck means you want them to join you for a drink. You only do this with close friends. In Russia giving someone a thumbs up and making a sprinkling motion over it means job well done. In India you say sorry by tapping someone on the shoulder and touching your forehead. In Turkey pretending to throw salt over your shoulder with an open palm means don't worry about it.

Just like words gestures have their own origins. But since gestures predate verbal communication and thus written record the origins are difficult to trace. This does not keep people from speculating. Here is a myth behind a common gesture; the Roman emperors thumbs down gesture telling the gladiator to finish off the other gladiator. Today's popular culture has it that a thumbs down meant death while a thumbs up would grant the loser his life. There is no evidence of this. In fact most scholars now believe that the finish him gesture was a thumbs up while a thumb hidden inside a fist spared the loser. This is not absolutely verified. However since the thumbs up was an insult in Roman times this makes more sense than the accepted folklore.

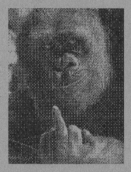

Primates, with the exception of humans, have much better cortical control over hand movements than over voice, which is mostly restricted to emotionall based sounds controlled by sub cortical structures. This means that early hominids would have been better at expressive, voluntary communication using hands

THE ORIGIN OF THE MIDDLE FINGER

well known & used all over the world but where does it actually come from?

In Western culture, the finger or the middle finger, as in giving someone the finger or the bird or flipping someone off, is the most obscene hand gesture. It communicates moderate to extreme contempt, and is roughly equivalent in meaning to "fuck off", "fuck you", "shove it up your ass", "up yours" or "go fuck yourself". It is performed by showing the back of a hand that has only the middle finger extended upwards, though in some locales the thumb is extended. Extending the finger is considered a symbol of contempt in several cultures, especially in the West. Many cultures use similar gestures to display their disrespect, although others use it to express pointing without intentional disrespect toward other cultures. The gesture is usually used to express contempt but can also be used humorously or playfully.

The gesture dates back to Ancient Greece and it was also used in Ancient Rome. Historically, it represented the phallus. In some modern cultures, it has gained increasing recognition as a sign of disrespect, and has been used by music artists (notably more common among hardcore punk bands and rappers), actors, celebrities, athletes, and politicians. Most still view the gesture as obscene. The index finger and ring finger besides the middle finger in more contemporary periods has been likened to represent the testicles.

1.Origin
1.1 Classical era

The middle finger gesture was used in Ancient times as a symbol of sexual intercourse, in a manner meant to de- grade, intimidate and threaten the individual receiving the gesture. It also represented the phallus, with the fingers next to the middle finger representing testicles; from its close association, the gesture may have assumed apotropaic potency. In the firs century Mediterranean world, extending the finger was one of many methods used to divert the ever-present threat of the evil eye. In ancient Greek comedy, the finger was a gesture of insult toward another person, with the term katapugon also referring to "a male who submits to anal penetration"or katapygaina to a female. In Aristophanes's comedy The Clouds,when the character Socrates is quizzing his student on poetic meters, Strepsiades declares that he knows quite well what a dactyl is, and gives the fin- ger. The gesture is a visual pun on the two meanings of the Greek word "dactylos", both "finger" and the rhythmic measure composed of a long syllable and two short, like the joints of a finger, which also appears as a visual pun on the penis and testicles in a medieval Latin text. Socrates reacts to the gesture as boorish and childish.The gesture recurs as a form of mockery in Peace, alongside farting in someone's face; the usage is later explained in the Suda and included in the Adagia of Erasmus. The verb "to play the Siphnian" appears in a fragment of Aristophanes and has a similar meaning; the usage is once again explained in the Suda, where it is said to mean "to touch the anus with a finger". Diogenes Laertius records how the Cynic philosopher Diogenes directed the gesture at the orator Demosthenes in 4th-century BC Athens. In the Discourses of Epictetus, Diogenes's target is instead one of the sophists.

In Latin, the middle finger was the digitus impudicus, meaning the "shameless, indecent or offensive finger". In the 1st century AD, Persius had superstitious female relatives concoct a charm with the "infamous finger", digitus infamis, and "purifying spit";while in the Satyricon, an old woman uses dust, spit and her middle finger to mark the forehead before casting a spell.The poet Martial has a character in good health ex- tend "the indecent one" toward three doctors.In another epigram, Martial wrote: "Laugh loud, Sextillus, at whoever calls you a cinaedus and extend your middle finger."Juvenal, through synecdoche, has the "middle nail" cocked at threatening Fortuna. The in- decent finger features again in a mocking context in the Priapeia, a collection of poems relating to the phallic god Priapus.In Late Antiquity, the term "shameless finger" is explained in the Etymologiae of Isidore of Seville with reference to its frequent use when accusing someone of a "shameful action".

1.2 Modern era (United States)

Linguist Jesse Sheidlower traces the gesture's development in the United States to the 1890s. According to anthropologist Desmond Morris, the gesture probably came to the United States via Italian immigrants. The first documented appearance of the finger in the United States was in 1886, when Old Hoss Radbourn, a baseball pitcher for the Boston Beaneaters, was photographed giving it to a member of their rival the New York Giants. In the film Speedy (1928), Harold Lloyd's character gives himself the finger into a distorting mirror at Luna Park, about 24 minutes into the film; the exact meaning in the film's context is not clear.

2.Cultural Impact
2.1 Politics and military incidents

The gesture has been involved in notable political events. During the USS Pueblo incident, in which an American ship was captured by North Korea, the captured American crewmembers often discreetly gave the finger in staged photo ops, thus ruining the North Koreans' efforts at propaganda. The North Koreans, ignorant of what the gesture meant, were at first told by the pris- oners that it was a "Hawaiian good luck sign", similar to "hang loose". When the guards finally figured things out, the crewmembers were subjected to more severe mistreatment. Abbie Hoffman used the gesture at the 1968 Democratic National Convention. Ronald Reagan, while serving as the Governor of California, gave the middle finger to counterculture protestors in Berkeley, California. Nelson Rockefeller, then the Vice President of the United States, directed the gesture to hecklers at a 1976 campaign stop near Binghamton, New York, leading it to be called the "Rockefeller gesture". Pierre Trudeau, then the Prime Minister of Canada, gave the finger to protesters in Salmon Arm, British Columbia, earning the incident the nickname the "Salmon Arm salute". The gesture itself has also

been nicknamed the "Trudeau salute". Former president George W. Bush gave the finger to the camera at an Austin production facility during his term as governor of Texas, saying it was "just a one finger victory salute." Anthony Weiner gave the finger to reporters after leaving his election headquarters the night he lost the 2013 primary election for Mayor of New York City.

During World War II, the 91st Bombardment Group of the United States Army Air Forces referred to the gesture as the "rigid digit" salute. It was used in a more jocular manner, to suggest an airman had committed an error or infraction; the term was a reference to British slang terms for inattentiveness (i.e. "pull your finger out (of your bum)"). The order of the rigid digit" continued after the war as a series of awards presented by the veteran's association of the 91st, marked by wooden statuettes of a hand giving the single finger gesture. In 2005 during the war in Iraq, Gunnery Sergeant Michael Burghardt gained prominence when the Omaha World Herald published a photo of Burghardt making the gesture towards Iraqi insurgents he believed to be watching after an improvised explosive device failed to kill him.

The middle finger has been involved in judicial hearings. An appellate court in Hartford, Connecticut ruled in 1976 that gesturing with the middle finger was offensive, but not obscene, after a police officer charged a 16 year old with making an obscene gesture when the student gave the officer the middle finger. The case was appealed to the Connecticut Supreme Court, which upheld the decision. In March 2006, a federal lawsuit was filed regarding the free speech issue.

Giving the finger has resulted in negative consequences. A Malaysian man was bludgeoned to death after giving the finger to a motorist following a car chase.A Pakistani man was deported by the United Arab Emirates for the gesture, which violates indecency codes.People have given the finger as a method of political protest. At a concert, Ricky Martin gave a picture of George W. Bush the finger to protest the War in Iraq. Serbian protesters gave the finger to the Russian embassy regarding their support of Slobodan Milosevic. Artist Ai Weiwei has used the finger in photographs and sculp- tures as a political statement. As a political message to the Czech President, Czech artist David Cerny floated an outsize, purple statue of a hand on the River Vltava in Prague; its middle finger extended towards Prague Castle, the Presidential seat.

2.2 In popular culture

The use of the middle finger has become pervasive in pop-ular culture. The band Cobra Starship released a song called "Middle Finger", and released a music video that showed people giving the finger. Italian artist Maurizio Cattelan installed a marble statue of a middle finger measuring 11 metres, located directly in front of the Milan Stock Exchange.A now famous photograph of Johnny Cash shows him giving the middle finger to a photographer during a 1969 concert at San Quentin State Prison, released as At San Quentin.However, the photo remained fairly obscure until 1998, when producer Rick Rubin made it the centerpiece of an ad in Billboard criticizing country radio for not giving airplay to Cash's Grammy winning album Unchained.Cameron Diaz made the gesture during a photo shoot for Esquire.Harold Lloyd shot the finger to his own reflection in a Coney Island funhouse after getting paint on his suit in Speedy, his final silent feature, from 1928.

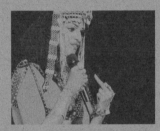

This is M.I.A. giving the gesture during the Super Bowl 2011 Halftime Show. This caused trouble. So the National Football League, NBC, and M.I.A. had to apologize

Athletes, including Stefan Effenberg, Ron Artest, Luis Suarez, Juan Pablo Montoya, Ivan Rodriguez, Danny Graves, Jack McDowell, Natasha Zvereva, Josh Smith, Bryan Cox, and Johnny Manziel have been suspended or fined for making the gesture. Jose Paniagua was released by the Chicago White Sox after giving the middle finger to an umpire; he hasn't played in the majors since. Baseball executive Chub Feeney once resigned after giving the finger to fans on Fan Appreciation Night.Bud Adams, owner of the National Football League's Tennessee Titans, was fined 250,000 dollar for giving both middle fingers to the fans of the Buffalo Bills during a game. Professional wrestler Stone Cold Steve Austin is also famous for flashing one or both middle fingers as part of his gimmick.

Many musical artists, including Madonna, Lady Gaga, Eminem, Katy Perry, and Adele have publicly made the gesture. Britney Spears and Iggy Azalea have given the gesture towards members of the paparazzi, but had to apologize when fans interpreted the gesture as directed at them. M.I.A. gave the gesture during the Super Bowl XLVI Halftime Show.The National Football League, NBC, and M.I.A. apologized.The CD itself for Kid Rock's album Devil Without a Cause is a picture of his raised middle finger. On the cover of Moby Grape's first album, Moby Grape, band member Don Stevenson was caught flipping the bird at the camera. The finger was airbrushed out of subsequent releases of the album. In auto-mobile driving culture, giving the finger to a fellow motorist communicates displeasure at another person's reckless driving habits and their disregard for common courtesy.

The media sometimes refers to the gesture as being mistaken for an indication of "we're number one", typically indicated with a raised index finger. Sometimes, though, the "mistake" is actually an intentional euphemism meant to indirectly convey the gesture in a medium where a direct description would be inappropriate. For example, Don Mer-edith is famously noted in a 1972 Monday Night Football game describing the Finger of a dejected Houston Oilers fan as, "He thinks they're number one in the nation." Ira Robbins, a law professor, believes the finger is no longer an obscene gesture. Psychologist David Walsh, founder of the National Institute on Media and the Family, sees the growing accep- tance of the middle finger as a sign of the growth of a "culture of disrespect".Google Street View's picture of the area around the Wisconsin Governor's Mansion, taken in 2011, shows a jogger giving the finger in the direction of the mansion.

3.Similar Gestures

In the United Kingdom, Ireland, Australia, and New Zealand, the V sign or "the fingers", when given with back of the hand towards the recipient, serves a similar purpose. George H. W. Bush, former President of the United States, accidentally made the gesture while on a diplomatic trip to Australia. In countries where Spanish, Portuguese, or French are spoken, and especially in Spain, Portugal, Brazil, France the gesture involves rais-ing a fist and slapping the biceps on the same arm as the fist used, sometimes called the Spanish slap, is equivalent to the finger. Italy, Poland, and coun-tries under the influence of Russian culture, such as Russia, Belarus, and Ukraine, also see it as equivalent to the finger, but the majority of young people in these countries use the finger as an insult, which is associated with the Western culture.

In Iran and Iraq, a gesture involving exposing only the thumb in a vertical orientation, a thumbs up, is used in lieu of the finger to express roughly the same sentiment. A similarly obscene gesture is extending all five digits with the palm facing forward, meaning "you have five fathers", thus calling someone a bastard. This is similar to a gesture known in Greece as the Moutza, where the five fingers are spread wide and the palm is pushed towards the recipient. More commonly in Turkish or Slavic regions, the fig sign serves as the equivalent to the finger, meaning "you won't get it", "in your dreams". The gesture is typically made with the hand and fingers curled and the thumb thrust between the middle and index fingers. This gesture is also used similarly in Indonesia, Turkey and China.In most Arabic speaking countries and in Israel, doing the opposite as the western style of the finger, so all fingers open with the middle finger down flat, not curled, and the palm is facing up.

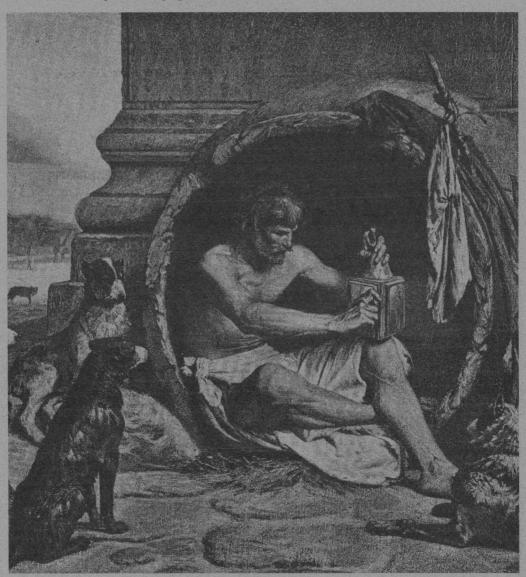

The Cynic philosopher Diogenes, pictured by Gerome with the large jar in which he lived; when strangers at the inn were expressing their wish to catch sight of the great orator Demosthenes, Diogenes is said to have stuck out his middle finger and exclaimed "this, for you, is the demagogue of the Athenians"

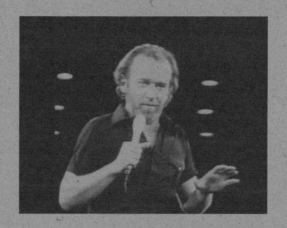

"**The original seven words were, shit, piss, fuck, cunt, cocksucker, motherfucker, and tits. Those are the ones that will curve your spine, grow hair on your hands and maybe, even bring us, God help us, peace without honor, and a bourbon.**"

George Carlin, „Filthy Words", 1972

SEVEN WORDS YOU CAN NEVER SAY ON TELEVISION

The transcript of Geore Carlin's famous monologue "Filthy Words"

I was thinking about the curse words and the swear words, the cuss words and the words that you can't say, that you're not supposed to say all the time, words or people into words want to hear your words. Some guys like to record your words and sell them back to you if they can, listen in on the telephone, write down what words you say. A guy who used to be in Washington knew that his phone was tapped, used to answer, Fuck Hoover, yes, go ahead. Okay, I was thinking one night about the words you couldn't say on the public, ah, airwaves, um, the ones you definitely wouldn't say, ever, cause I heard a lady say bitch one night on television, and it was cool like she was talking about, you know, ah, well, the bitch is the first one to notice that in the litter Johnie right Right. And, uh, bastard you can say, and hell and damn so I have to figure out which ones you couldn't and ever and it came down to seven but the list is open to amendment, and in fact, has been changed, uh, by now, ha, a lot of people pointed things out to me, and I noticed some myself. The original seven words were, shit, piss, fuck, cunt, cocksucker, motherfucker, and tits. Those are the ones that will curve your spine, grow hair on your hands and maybe, even bring us, God help us, peace without honor, and a bourbon. And now the first thing that we noticed was that word fuck was really repeated in there because the word motherfucker is a compound word and it's another form of the word fuck. You want to be a purist it doesn't really it can't be on the list of basic words. Also, cocksucker is a compound word and neither half of that is really dirty. The word the half sucker that's merely suggestive and the word cock is a halfway dirty word, 50 percent dirty ,dirty half the time, depending on what you mean by it. Uh, remember when you first heard it, like in 6th grade, you used to giggle. And the cock crowed three times, heh the cock three times. It's in the Bible, cock in the Bible. And the first time you heard about a cock-fight, remember What? Huh? naw. It ain't that, are you stupid? man. It's chickens, you know, Then you have the four letter words from the old Anglo-Saxon fame. Uh, shit and fuck. The word shit, uh, is an interesting kind of word in that the middle class has never really accepted it and approved it. They use it like, crazy but it's not really okay. It's still a rude, dirty, old kind of gushy word. They don't like that, but they say it, like, they say it like, a lady now in a middle-class home, you'll hear most of the time she says it as an expletive, you know, it's out of her mouth before she knows. She says, Oh shit oh shit, oh shit. If she drops something, Oh, the shit hurt the broccoli. Shit. Thank you.

Shit! I won the Grammy, man, for the comedy album. Isn't that groovy? That's true. Thank you. Thank you man. Yeah. Thank you man. Thank you. Thank you very much, man. Thank, no, for that and for the Grammy, man, cause that's based on people liking it man, yeh, that's ah, that's okay man. Let's let that go, man. I got my Grammy. I can let my hair hang down now, shit. Ha! So! Now the word shit is okay for the man. At work you can say it like crazy. Mostly figuratively, Get that shit out of here, will ya? I don't want to see that shit anymore. I can't cut that shit, buddy. I've had that shit up to here. I think you're full of shit myself. He don't know shit from Shinola. you know that? Always wondered how the Shinola people feel about that Hi, I'm the new man from Shinola. Hi, how are ya? Nice to see ya. How are ya? Boy, I don't know whether to shit or wind my watch. Guess, I'll shit on my watch. Oh, the shit is going to hit de fan. Built like a brick shit-house. Up, he's up shit's creek. He's had it. He hit me, I'm sorry. Hot shit, holy shit, tough shit, eat shit, shit-eating grin. Uh, whoever thought of that was ill. He had a shit eating grin! He had a what? Shit on a stick. Shit in a handbag. I always like that. He ain't worth shit in a handbag. Shitty. He acted real shitty. You know what I mean? I got the money back, but a real shitty attitude.

Heh, he had a shit-fit. Wow! Shit fit. Whew! Glad I wasn't there. All the animals   Bull shit, horse shit, cow shit, rat shit, bat shit. First time I heard bat shit, I really came apart. A guy in Oklahoma, Boggs, said it, man. Aw! Bat shit. Vera reminded me of that last night, ah. Snake shit, slicker than owl shit. Get your shit together. Shit or get off the pot. I got a shitload full of them. I got a shitpot full, all right. Shithead, shitheel, shit in your heart, shit for brains, shitface, heh I always try to think how that could have originated; the first guy that said that. Somebody got drunk and fell in some shit, you know. Hey, I'm shitface. Shitface, today. Anyway, enough of that shit.

The big one, the word fuck that's the one that hangs them up the most. Cause in a lot of cases that's the very act that hangs them up the most. So, it's natural that the word would, uh, have the same effect. It's a great word, fuck, nice word, easy word, cute word, kind of. Easy word to say. You know, it's easy. Starts with a nice soft sound fuh ends with a kuh. Right? A little something for everyone. Fuck Good word. Kind of a proud word, too. Who are you? I am *fuck fuck of the muntain.* Tune in again next week to *Fuck of the mountain*. It's an interesting word too, cause it's got a double kind of a life personality dual, you know, whatever the right phrase is. It leads a double life, the word fuck. First of all, it means, sometimes, most of the time, fuck. What does it mean? It means to make love. Right? We're going to make love, yeh, we're going to fuck, yeh, we're going to fuck, yeh, we're going to make love. we're really going to fuck, yeah, we're going to make love. Right? And it also means the beginning of life, it's the act that begins life, so there's the word hanging around with words like love, and life, and yet on the other hand, it's also a word that we really use to hurt each other with, man. It's a heavy. It's one that you have toward the end of the argument. Right? You finally can't make out. Oh, fuck you man. I said, fuck you. Stupid fuck. Fuck you and everybody

that looks like you. man. It would be nice to change the movies that we already have and substitute the word fuck for the word kill, wherever we could, and some of those movie cliches would change a little bit. Madfuckers still on the loose. Stop me before I fuck again. Fuck the ump, fuck the ump, fuck the ump, fuck the ump, fuck the ump. Easy on the clutch Bill, you'll fuck that engine again. The other shit one was, I don't give a shit. Like it's worth something, you know? I don't give a shit. Hey, well, I don't take no shit, you know what I mean? You know why I don't take no shit? Cause I don't give a shit. If I give a shit, I would have to pack shit. But I don't pack no shit cause I don't give a shit. You wouldn't shit me, would you? That's a joke when you're a kid with a worm looking out the bird's ass. You wouldn't shit me, would you? It's an eight-year-old joke but a good one. The additions to the list. I found three more words that had to be put on the list of words you could never say on television, and they were fart, turd and twat, those three. Fart, we talked about, it's harmless It's like tits, it's a cutie word, no problem. Turd, you can't say but who wants to, you know?

The subject never comes up on the panel so I'm not worried about that one. Now the word twat is an interesting word. Twat! Yeh, right in the twat. Twat is an interesting word because it's the only one I know of, the only slang word applying to the, a part of the sexual anatomy that doesn't have another meaning to it. Like, ah, snatch, box and pussy all have other meanings, man. Even in a Walt Disney movie, you can say, We're going to snatch that pussy and put him in a box and bring him on the airplane. Everybody loves it. The twat stands alone, man, as it should. And two-way words. Ah, ass is okay providing you're riding into town on a religious feast day. You can't say, up your ass. You can say, stuff it! There are certain things you can say its weird but you can just come so close. Before I cut, I, uh, want to, ah, thank you for listening to my words, man, fellow, uh space travelers. Thank you man for tonight and thank you also.

THE SCIENCE OF SWEARING

A look into the human mind & other less socially acceptable four letter words by Michelle Drews

What's in a word? Would that which I call my pen write any less well if I call it a banana? Would it taste any better? A core tenant of linguistics is the idea that words are merely a collection of syllables associated with ideas, yet most words are more than just their literal meanings, they also carry an emotional connotation as a result of how they are used within the language. For some words, this emotional connotation is so intense that that, even in a country like the United States, where freedom of speech is a fundamental tenant, the use of these words can be officially banned.

The consequences of using them in an "inappropriate" context can range from censorship and fines to ostracism and the loss of your cooking show. In spite of this, swear words, taboo phrases, and other forms of curses persist across societies and throughout history, a product of culture, language, and the brain itself.

Becoming Taboo

When asked to define profanity in 1964, former Supreme Court Justice Potter Stewart famously stated that he could not describe it and added, "But I know it when I see it" (Jacobellis v. Ohio, 1964). Though the material in question was pornography, the difficulty of a universal definition extends into profane language as well. While there are some qualifications that extend to all swear words, the magnitude of "offensiveness" can vary greatly, making a precise, literal definition of the word challenging. Most swear words and taboo phrases tend to deal with material that is offensive in some manner. Studies of swear words have shown that the most common swear words can be categorized as deistic, visceral, or social. In particular, studies show that sex related insults in particular are common across cultures.

However, simply referring to sex or genitalia is not sufficient to make a word or phrase taboo. Our reaction to the word "fuck" is much different than our reaction to "coitus," "make love," or even "have sex." There is also nothing special about the sounds or syllables in the word "fuck." Close-sounding words, such as "duck," "truck," and "buck", are not prohibited and in some cases can serve as a more socially appropriate substitution for what everyone understands was meant to be a curse word, for example "mothertrucker!" How then does a word become taboo? Since taboos are cultural concepts, the answer must be through society. The word taboo is defined as "a social or religious custom prohibiting or forbidding discussion of a particular practice or forbidding association with a particular person, place, or thing". First, taboos must be internalized by an individual, usually in childhood, along with many other social norms and customs.

This early acquisition of taboos is evident in studies of individuals who acquired a second language later in life. These individuals react much more strongly to swear words in their first language than in their second. As children, we are punished by caregivers such as parents when we swear, and through aversive conditioning we learn that certain phrases are to be avoided. Later, when we mature, we learn the complex social features and characteristics that underlie certain taboos; thus, a more nuanced understanding of where and when to avoid taboo phrases develops.Furthermore, as culture changes, so does what is taboo.

The words "gay" and "nigger" both provide excellent examples. While the word "nigger" used to be considered socially acceptable in many circles, now it is considered a highly offensive term thanks to more modern thinking and the civil rights movement. The word "gay," originally meaning "extremely happy," is now associated with homosexuality and can carry a number of different connotations depending on who is using it, and in what context.

Why Swear?

So, if taboo phrases are cultural no-nos, why do they persist? The simplest answer is that in certain situations swear words and taboo phrases have their uses: mainly to evoke a strong negative reaction from someone. Speech perception is nearly automatic in mature individuals. Try this: don't think of an apple. Did you think of an apple anyway when you read the word "apple"? With swear words, your mind immediately drags up whatever offensive combination of denotations and connotations are associated with the word in question when you hear it. These make swear words powerful insults and forceful descriptors of the nastier aspects of things we may not want to think about.

Swear words are also useful and effective ways of conveying that you feel very strongly about something or of inciting strong feelings in someone else, even when used outside of their traditional definitions. Saying that something is "bloody amazing" does not mean that that thing was literally bloody, but adding the term "bloody" to the phrase gives it extra emotional emphasis.

However, swearing is not always about evoking negative emotions; swearing itself can also be a cultural phenomenon. The willingness to break a cultural taboo in front of others creates an atmosphere of informality and sense of community. If taboos are defined by the greater society, an environment where subverting those taboos is acceptable creates a smaller, more intimate society inside of the greater society. Another interesting use of taboo language is as a cathartic experience, a way of expressing and alleviating pain, frustration, stress, or regret. A classic example of this would be shouting "damn it" after hitting yourself with a hammer while trying to nail something down. Interestingly, studies have shown that, when compared with people who do not swear frequently, frequent swearers also tend to have lower pain tolerance. Swearing was also shown to increase the ability of subjects to tolerate pain. All of these uses contribute to the propagation of swear words and taboo phrases in language, despite their inappropriateness in certain contexts.

Swearing in the Brain

In an effort to understand how swearing provokes a strong response in individuals, neuroscientists looked to the brain for answers. Using neuroimaging techniques such as PET (positron emission tomography) scans, they demonstrated that a small part of the brain called the amygdala is highly active when exposed to threatening words (Isenberg, 1999). The amygdala is part of the limbic system, one of the primitive parts of the brain responsible for processing emotion and memory. In particular, amygdala activity is correlated with negative emotional associations; stimulating the amygdala can cause panic attacks and aggressive behaviors, while destroying the amygdala causes unusual placidness or fearlessness. Therefore, it makes sense that the amygdala would be activated in association with unpleasant words such as swear words. The amygdala also makes several connections to memory and association centers in the brain, which could also be responsible for the increased memory skills when subjects are presented with swear words.

Swearing in the Clinic

Beyond simply determining what part of the brain is activated, neuroscientists also sought insight into how swear words are produced in the brain by looking to the clinic. Pathological swearing is found in many neurolinguistic disorders, the most famous being Gilles de la Tourette syndrome. GTS, which was first identified by Itard and Gilles de la Tourette in the 1800s, is a hyperkinetic motor speech disorder characterized by frequent involuntary "tics," which are sudden pattern-like movements or sounds. In most popculture portrayals of Tourette's, corpolalia, or involuntary swearing, features very prominently. In GTS individuals with corpolalia, swearing is a tic. However, despite the prevalence of corpolalia in media depictions, only about 10 to 25 percent of individuals with Tourette syndrome exhibit corpolalia. Though it is lesser known than Tourette syndrome, aphasia can also heavily feature swearing. Aphasia is a clinical language impairment resulting from damage to the language centers of the brain, usually following a stroke. The exact specifics of a particular aphasia depend on the location and severity of the damage; in general, though, aphasic individuals have problems with speech, listening, reading, and writing. In the most severe case, global aphasia, speech is almost nonexistent. Yet, in numerous cases these individuals are still able to swear normally Even in individuals with less extensive aphasias, where speech is possible but difficult, limited, and often incorrectly pronounced, patients have been known to use swear words easily with the proper pronunciation. For example, R.N., a patient with global aphasia as a result of a stroke involving his left frontal, temporal and parietal lobes, could only say "well," "yeah," "yes," "no," "goddammit," and "shit". Patient R.N. was able to produce these words properly in the proper context, however, when asked to say the word "shit" out of conversational context by reading it from a written card, he was unable to do so.

The use of swearing in both aphasia and GTS gives us a real insight into how swearing works in the brain. Individuals with aphasia have damage to the normal parts of the brain that produce formal language, such as Broca's area or Wernicke's area, found in the left hemisphere of the brain. The fact that they are able to swear suggests that swearing is localized outside of these damaged areas and is handled differently in the brain than other parts of language. Psychologist Chris Code, who studied individuals who had their left hemispheres removed, proposed that swear words and several other types of speech preserved in aphasic individuals fall into a category of "lexical automatisms" or automatic speech, which are localized to the right hemisphere instead of the left one

Pathological and neuroimaging studies of individuals with Tourette syndrome implicate the basal ganglia and the limbic system as key players in GTS and corpolalia. The basal ganglia have several main roles in the brain, including the regulation of actions, and use dopamine as their main neurotransmitter. Parkinson's disease and Huntington's disease are two classic examples of basal ganglia dysfunction. In Parkinson's disease, the basal ganglia are damaged in such a way that they inhibit motor signals coming from the cortex, and thus movement is very difficult. In Huntington's disease, the basal ganglia are damaged in just the opposite fashion, they do not inhibit motor signals like they normally would, and patients move unintentionally and uncontrollably. If we consider speech as just another type of movement that can either be suppressed or released by the basal ganglia, it makes sense that they would be involved in swearing, keeping taboo ideas that cross our thoughts from being expressed more fully. This is a useful tool for the brain because, to quote Harvard Psychologist Steven Pinker, "you have to think the unthinkable to know what you're not supposed to be thinking". Though studies of GTS individuals show a high level of variability in the brain areas they implicate, the

basal ganglia and dopamine system in particular have been shown to be dysfunctional in many studies. Dopamine antagonists, drugs that block or lower the effects of dopamine receptor signaling, have also proven effective in alleviating some GTS symptoms, further supporting the idea that the basal ganglia are involved in GTS.

The limbic system, which includes the amygdala, also has a variety of other roles, most of which involve emotion. Important to the topic of swearing, the limbic system has been shown to be important in the production of emotional language.Therefore, one theory is that dysfunction in the limbic system and basal ganglia can produce corpolalia, which stems from a loss of inhibitory ability coupled with high emotional reactivity. These two areas are also usually intact after an aphasic stroke, meaning that the ability to swear should also be preserved. Still, we do not have all the answers yet, there are exceptions and inconsistencies in every case. Nevertheless, these findings may give us the beginnings of an understanding of how swearing works in the brain.

Sticks and Stones
Free Speech and Words that hurt

Though understanding how swearing works in the brain is a puzzle that scientists will keep working on, the far more controversial question about swear words is how we should deal with them legislatively. Freedom of speech, the first and foremost Amendment in the Bill of Rights, is seen as one of the founding tenants of a democratic society. However, there are cases of what the Supreme Court calls "unprotected speech" where speech can be restricted. Slander, libel, and "fighting words" are all examples of unprotected speech. In each of these cases, the speech has been deemed harmful to others and is therefore illegal.Obscenity is also considered a type of unprotected speech, under the argument that offensive words also constitute a form of harm, particularly for the vulnerable and the young. This idea has been the basis of many of the rules enforced by the Federal Communications Commission, which has fined TV stations and Radio Networks for everything from broadcasting George Carlin's "Seven Words You Can Never Say on Television" to Bono's fleeting use of "fucking brilliant" at the Golden Globe Awards. Yet, are offensive words actually harmful? Psychological studies have shown that context is essential in terms of harmful speech. On one hand, a study of child victims of obscene telephone calls showed that the children suffered severe psychological consequences from these calls. Verbal harassment and aggression has also been shown to have clear negative psychological effects. On the other hand, the evidence against swearing alone is much less compelling. As discussed above, there are many psychological studies that suggest swear words, in the appropriate context, can be beneficial when used for group unity, coherence, and general expressiveness

This is not to say that the use of swear words and taboo phrases is totally without potentially harmful consequences; just ask Paula Deen. In most instances, these words are taboo for a reason. Usually, they are considered offensive in one way or the other and evoke strong emotions, or strong amygdala reactivity, which can be harmful to relationships and other social constructs. However, the question of whether these social harms are sufficient punishment for the use of offensive language or if legislative action must be taken as well remains within the courts and legislators' discretion Taboo language is defined by culture and is created in the brain through a complex interaction of our speech, emotion, and motivation centers. There are a variety of uses for it, and from a legal standpoint the context of use is everything when determining what is or is not appropriate. While we may not have all of the answers about the science behind swearing just yet, swear words have been a unique feature of language for across cultures and time, showing no signs of leaving anytime soon.

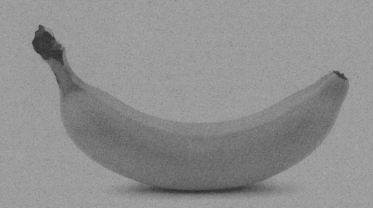

"What's in a word? Would that, which I call my pen, write any less well if I call it a banana? Would it taste any better?"

WHY WE CURSE

Extract of the Psycho Social Theory of Speech by Dr. Timothy Jay

While curse words can be differentiated from noncurse words through a social historical analysis, an act of cursing cannot be understood without considering simultaneously all three of the dimensions underlying human behavior. The NPS Theory is meant to explain why people curse and why they choose the words they do. The Theory integrates previous historical, social, and psychological approaches in order to represent cursing as the product of three interdependent systems.

In the NPS Theory, the historical-social information about word use is subsumed by the sociocultural system. The sociocultural system describes variables, such as humor elicitation, that a speaker uses to determine if a word is appropriate in a given context or not. Each culture has developed its own criteria for what constitutes a good, funny dirty joke. What makes a dirty joke inappropriate or unfunny depends on the joke and the context (the office versus the local pub). The point is that offensiveness and humor depend on cultural contexts .The linguistic and semantic analysis of a curse word's use is subsumed by the psychological system in NPS. In the psychological system, it is assumed that a speaker acquires linguistic competence and exhibits linguistic performance as the result of psychological development within a sociocultural language context. Different cultures and different languages, of course, present different sets of linguistic and semantic constraints on dirty word use. This is to say that although individual speakers in one society might learn to speak the dominant language, each person ,s use of curse words is determined by his or her psychological development within a given linguistic, familial, and cultural environment. Psychological development includes variables thatdirectly affect cursing, such as temperament, personality traits, religiosity, social rewards, and punishments.

Underlying the broad sociocultural system in which each person is subject to psychological restraints is a developing brain .The developing brain is a neurological system of control processes.

It is essentially similar in all healthy infants, regardless of the cultural context or the language to be learned. In the NPS, two interlocking neural systems are important: (a) the cerebral cortex, which governs speech comprehension and production, and (b) the subcortical systems (limbic system, basal ganglia, and amygdala), which regulate emotion al reactions such as approach-avoidance responses. These two brain systems playa central role in regulating a speaker's verbal expressions, so that a person , s emotional responses occur at different levels of awareness and controllability. Cursing may take the form of an automatic reflex (outside of awareness and difficult to control) or a more complex, strategic, controlled response. Finally, we can observe how cursing is controlled by the brain systems by observing brain damaged speakers whose cursing behavior s are compared to normal speakers cursing.

The NPS Theory is designed to account for all cursing behaviors in all social and cultural contexts over the course of an individual's psychological development. The NPS Theory provides a three-dimensional model of a person's knowledge of cursing, which develops as a person matures. An individual' s knowledge depends on personal experience, psychological makeup: and on the culture in which he or she is raised. As such, a person's style of cursing will be the product of both shared and private experiences.

Past research provides some historical and psychological insight into why people curse. But the neurological level is where we have the most to learn about cursing.We need to look thoroughly at emotion states and how subcortical brain structures affect cursing. The brain is viewed as a storehouse of psychological and sociocultural information that is used to determine how to curse appropriately, that is, when the psychological and social factors require cursing.The three systems in the NPS Theory are viewed as interlocking systems. One system might predominate over another system in a given situation to produce a cursing episode, but each system has some input into the production of the cursing episodes. The psychological level presumes a neurological level; that is, a brain develops within a person. The sociocultural system accounts for the context in which the person develops and the social factors that affect cursing in public. Cultural factors include religion, taboos, gender identification, censorship, and social power. The social level presumes psychological and neurological levels; that is, a brain in a person develops in a cultural context that defines and proscribes acts of cursing.

The NPS Theory can be conceptualized as three intersecting spheres of influence. An act of cursing is instigated by factors involved within one or more of these spheres. For example, Broca's patient, Leborgne, who could only say "Sacre nom de Dieu!", was dominated by his neurological sphere. Neurological control predominates in the cry from an Alzheimer disease victim or a Touretter. An infant mimicking a parent's swearing is primarily using the neurological and psychological spheres, with little influence from the sociocultural level. Telling a novel and clever dirty joke is the product of all three spheres.

The NPS Theory is designed to account for why a speaker does or does not curse in a particular context. The way in which the brain moderates behavior is of growing interest, in this case , how the cortical and subcortical areas represent curse words and produce cursing in emotional expressions. The brain responds to a range of emotional information; some responses are reflexive and others are voluntary. Emotional expressions draw words from a cursing lexicon, or cursing module, in the cortex. Curse words are embedded in the semantic neural network that develops and expands with experience. The neural network approach to speech and memory proces ses is referred to as a connectionist model or as parallel distributed processes. It has become increasingly popular to use this approach to describe language processes, and the approach is also applicable to cursing, if curse words are described as part of a network of concepts. The NPS Theory has both explanatory and predictive power. It explains how and why a speaker uses curse words in a sample of speech. The NPS Theory also predicts the conditions under which speakers in a culture are likely to use curse words. The ultimate form of the cursing episo des depend on a speaker's psychological development and the social context in which he or she operates. The NPS Theory accounts for why a person might swear in one context but not another. For example, lover s use vulgar sexual terms in the bedroom for purposes of enticement, but they never utter these words in public.

For the NPS Theory, cursing is never chaotic, meamngless, or random behavior cursing is seen as purposeful and rule-governed. The goal of the NPS Theory is to generate likelihood "rules" that underline concepts of appropriateness, offensiveness, and humor. Discovering and testing these cursing rules is meant to give the Theory predictive power. The more accurately the NPS Theory can predict acts of cursing , the more valid is our understanding of cursing. Acquiring language means acquiring information about when and where to curse and what to say. One set of likelihood rules is psychological in nature; another is social. Each system in the NPS Theory is a set of production rules for cursing. Psychological and social rules can be congruent or they can conflict. For example, although it is inappropriate to use obscenities in a classroom, a child with an impulsive personality will ignore the social rule. This set of cursing rules represe nts a "grammar" of cursing that generates instances of cursing.

As cursing rules are developed, violations to the rules can be studied. Any number of utterances can be examined to determine if they are "ungrammatical" according to the Theory. The NPS grammar can also be used to study bilingual cursing, for example, how foreig n speakers acquire the rules of cursing in English. As a rule governed, grammatical system, the NPS Theory can be integrated into popular theories of speech production and comprehension. The goals of the NPS Theory are: (a) to promote a broader understanding of the essential role of cursing in human communication; (b) to promote the integration of cursing knowledge into theories of language in lingui stics and psychology; and (c) to stimulate research and discussion of cursing in pertinent professional literature. At an applied level, a better understanding of cursing will assist professionals in the social sciences to ameliorate contemporary social/legal problems caused by cursing, such as . sexual harassment in the workplace. As conceived here , the development and growth of the NPS Theory will promote a basic understanding of the phenomenon that can be applied to real world speech problems.[...]

A CONVERSATION WITH DR. AMAN

David Templeton talks to Maledictologist and editor of Maledicta Magazine Dr. Aman

"This is the first interview I've given in five years," smiles Dr. Reinhold Aman, ushering me into his book lined, box filled Santa Rosa home. "I'm a private person. I don't seek the spotlight." During our chat, he is softspoken and grandfatherly, his voice barely more than a whisper. He chuckles often. "And of course," he adds with a grin, "I've been in prison".

Now, there's a line that could either start a conversation or stop it cold. "I'm not ashamed of it," he says. "I committed no crime. I was just trying to get rid of a horrible judge and a slimebag lawyer, and I stepped on one too many legal dicks."

Dr. Aman is the one time professor of medieval literature who became an editorial force of nature with his eye-opening book series Maledicta: The International Journal of Verbal Aggression. With subscribers in nearly every nation on the planet, and with such fans as Stanley Kubrick and George Carlin to sing his praises, Aman has carved out a singular reputation as the world's most scholarly dirty old man.

Once called the "Noah Webster of verbal aggression" by the Chicago Tribune, Aman has long known the explosive nature of words. But even he was surprised when his colorfully titled, self-published pamphlet Legal Scumbags of Wisconsin was interpreted by a grand jury as constituting a physical threat against that aforementioned judge, who had ruled unfavorably against him when Aman lived in Wisconsin. Aman was threatened with 25 years in jail and ended up serving 22 months. "So I went to jail for using language a little too effectively," he says, laughing. "And now I can call myself a 'jolly good felon'. One thing the establishment can't handle is honesty. They say, 'Tell the truth, and the truth will set you free' but in Hungary there is a much better saying. Tell the truth and they will smash your head in!'" Aman has spent the months since his release reorganizing his publishing business and preparing for the release of Maledicta 11 and the compendium volume Opus Maledictorum: A Book of Bad Words

Maledicta 11 is the long-awaited follow-up to Maledicta 10 (published in 1990), and is being snapped up by long-deprived fans. Opening with Aman's scathingly angry (and very funny) "Open Letter to Janet Reno," the mail-order book contains dozens of short works on the etymology and social impact of everything from bathroom graffiti and dirty jokes to racial slurs and blasphemies.

Opus Maledictorum is a mesmerizing sampling of essays previously published in the journal. An excellent starting point for newcomers to the often-shocking world of verbal aggression, the collection contains such vocabulary-building essays as "Elementary Russian Obscenity," "A Taxonomy of the Provenance of Metaphorical Terms of Abuse," "I Wanna Hot Dog for My Roll: Suggestive Song Titles," and "Tom, Dick and Hairy: Notes on Genital Pet Names." Most of the contributors hold Ph.D.s and enjoy international academic respect in their fields. Authors include Dr. Rasmus Fog, Lois Monteiro, filmmaker John Hughes, and Aman himself, who writes with clear, scholarly efficiency while displaying a fondness for puns and a sharp, salty sense of humor.

"Most of my work does not deal with obscenity as such, with sex and scatology and all that," Aman explains, when asked what would drive a kindly old gentleman to peruse dictionaries all day in the search for dirty words. "Obscenity is less than two percent of what I do. I'm interested in verbal aggression. Anything negative. Unfortunately, it's the vulgarity that gets all the attention. If I never have to write about ,fuck, ,shit, and cocksucker again, I'm happy. But I record it all honestly."

"White Anglo Saxon Protestant mentality is very uptight when it comes to sex and excrement, body parts and bodily functions. The American 'dirty dozen', those words that are supposedly so scandalous, are extremely boring. If you want colorful insults, both the clean ones and the really nasty ones, you have to look to other cultures. I've done research in about 220 languages, and I've heard just about everything you can think of."

Some examples, perhaps? "Well, in Thailand," he complies, "they might say,'Talking to you is like playing a violin to a water buffalo', what a beautiful image. Some of the best are Yiddish insults. They are very clever. 'May you inherit three ships of gold and may it not be enough to pay your doctors' bills."

"In Spain and the other Catholic countries, they use a lot of blasphemy, in the same way we might use body parts. Sometimes the two cultures merge and you hear something like ,By the 24 balls of the 12 apostles of Christ!' Other cultures might use family members in their insults. One insult I heard from a Muslim Gypsy was, ,I fuck the soul of your dead mother!'" Aman grins. "That one combines everything, doesn't it? I get goosebumps!" He goes on to discuss the novelty of animal affronts, listing such insulting comparisons as ,snake, rat, and ,barracuda. "That last one is a good insult for a lawyer," he deadpans. "All of these words are very powerful," he continues. "I read a story in the newspaper recently. There was a guy who was robbing a bank in San Francisco. Now if he had just walked up to the teller and said, ,Give me all the money,' she would have given it to him and he would have taken off. But he said, ,Give me all the fuckin' money!' and this elderly bank teller was so upset that he had used that word she took the till and hit him over the head with it. The cops came and took him away. "This is something I know firsthand. I used a few words like that, and look what happened to me." he laughs.

"So I went to jail for using language a little too effectively and now I can call myself a, jolly good felon. One thing the establishment can't handle is honesty"

Reinhold Aman

SWEARING AS A RESPONSE TO PAIN

An Experiment by Richard Stephens, John Atkins and Andrew Kingston

Although a common pain response, whether swearing alters individuals experience of pain has not been investigated. This study investigated whether swearing affects cold pressor pain tolerance (the ability to withstand immersing the hand in icy water), pain perception and heart rate. In a repeated measures design, pain outcomes were assessed in participants asked to repeat a swear word versus a neutral word. In addition, sex differences and the roles of pain catastrophising, fear of pain and trait anxiety were explored. Swearing increased pain tolerance, increased heart rate and decreased perceived pain compared with not swearing. However, swearing did not increase pain tolerance in males with a tendency to catastrophise. The observed pain lessening (hypoalgesic) effect may occur because swearing induces a fight or flight response and nullifies the link between fear of pain and pain perception.

Introduction

Swearing, the use of offensive or obscene language, occurs in most human cultures. People swear to let off steam, to shock or insult, or out of habit. Cathartic swearing may occur in painful situations, for example giving birth or hitting one's thumb with a hammer. Swearing is also one symptom of the disinhibition in frontal lobe syndrome. For example, the famous frontal lobe patient Phineas P. Gage is said to have become 'fitful, irreverent, indulging at times in the grossest profanity'. Anecdotally (we found no supporting evidence in the literature), some pain theorists view swearing as a sign of 'pain-related catastrophising', which may be defined as a maladaptive response in which negative and unhelpful thoughts and ideas are brought to bear when pain is experienced. We wondered why swearing, a supposedly maladaptive response to pain, is such a common pain response.

Given that pain sensation can be affected by a variety of factors, such as attention state, emotional context, suggestions, attitudes, expectations and sensory information we carried out an experiment to test the as yet unvalidated hypothesis that swearing, being a maladaptive response to pain, would decrease pain tolerance and increase pain perception compared with not swearing. Participants were asked for 'five words you might use after hitting yourself on the thumb with a hammer' and used the first swear word on the list. As a control they were asked for 'five words to describe a table' and used the word whose position corresponded with the swear word. The 'cold pressor' paradigm was employed. This laboratory procedure requires participants to submerge one hand in ice-cold water until discomfort necessitates removal. Submersion latency is recorded as an index of pain tolerance. After each trial we measured heart rate to assess autonomic arousal and pain perception to provide an additional pain outcome variable. A repeated measures design was applied owing to its superior statistical power and to control group differences with regard to several pertinent factors. These were pain-related catastrophising defined above, fear of pain, the tendency to be afraid of pain and physical harm and trait anxiety, the long-term tendency to feel uneasy, afraid or worried. These factors, which are correlated with pain outcomes, were incorporated as covariates in some of the statistical analyses employed. The participants were 67 undergraduates. The Keele University School of Psychology Research Ethics Committee approved the study.

Design

Repeated measures; cold pressor latency, perceived pain and change in heart rate were compared across swearing and control conditions. Condition order was randomized across participants. Participants were asked to maintain a similar pace and volume of word recital across conditions.

Procedure

Participants individually attended a research laboratory. At the outset they were informed that the study was concerned with quantifying the degree of stress that various forms of language elicit during tense situations. Participants submerged their nondominant hand in the room temperature water for 3 min before each cold-pressor trial to create a standardized starting point. Then the participants immersed the same hand in the cold water with the instruction that they should submerge their unclenched hand for as long as they could, while repeating their chosen word. Timing began when the hand was fully immersed and stopped when the hand was fully removed from the water. A five minute time limit was imposed; ten participants reached this limit in one or both trials. One participant was excluded because none of their suggested words were swear words. Participants immersed the hand in the room temperature bath before the second and final trial. Heart rate was recorded after the initial hand submersion in the room temperature bath (resting heart rate) and at the end of each cold-pressor submersion. The Pain Catastrophising Questionnaire, the Spielberger State-Trait Anxiety Index and the Fear of Pain Questionnaire Version three were administered at the start of the test session; the Perceived Pain Scale was administered immediately after each cold-pressor submersion.

Results

All variables followed a normal distribution although tending towards platykurtotis in some cases. However, where appropriate transforms could be identified, analyses yielded identical results and so only nontransformed analyses are reported. A series of 22 mixed analysis of variances were used to investigate the effect of swearing and sex on cold-pressor latency, perceived pain scale score and change in heart rate. For cold-pressor latency there were main effects of swearing and sex, but no interaction. Latencies were longer in the swearing condition relative to the nonswearing condition, and in males relative to females.

For perceived pain, the swearing by sex interaction was significant and there was a main effect of swearing. Although both sexes experienced a reduction in perceived pain in the swearing condition, females did so to a greater extent. For heart rate, the swearing by sex interaction was significant as were the main effects of swearing and sex.

Swearing increased heart rate in both the sexes, but more so for females compared with males. Separate and simultaneous general linear model analyses were applied to each of the dependant variables: cold pressor latency, perceived pain scale score and change in heart rate. Each analysis included the qualitative predictors: swearing and sex, as well as one of the following centred quantitative predictors: catastrophising, fear of pain, or trait anxiety. In each analysis, to check regression homogeneity, first the three way interaction was examined in a GLM additionally containing all the two-way interactions and the main effects.

Where none of the interactions was significant, a final GLM including only the main effects, equivalent to traditional analysis of covariance, was applied. Before conducting the GLM analyses the correlations between the three covariates were calculated. Catastrophising was correlated with fear of pain and with trait anxiety. Trait anxiety and fear of pain were not correlated.

The three way interaction of swearing, sex and catastrophising was a significant predictor of cold-pressor latency Catastrophising predicted decreased latency in swearing males but not in nonswearing males or females. Catastrophising did not predict perceived pain or change in heart rate. The fear of pain by sex interaction predicted cold-pressor latency. Fear of pain predicted decreased latency in males but not females. The fear of pain by swearing interaction predicted perceived pain. Fear of pain predicted perceived pain in the nonswearing condition but not in the swearing condition. Fear of pain did not predict change in heart rate. Trait anxiety predicted change in heart rate but not coldpressor latency or perceived pain.

Discussion

This experiment tested the hypothesis that swearing, an assumed maladaptive pain response, would decrease pain tolerance and increase pain perception compared with not swearing. In fact, the opposite occurred, people withstood a moderately to strongly painful stimulus for significantly longer if they repeated a swear word rather than a nonswear word. Swearing also lowered pain perception and was accompanied by increased heart rate. We interpret these data as indicating that swearing, rather than being a maladaptive pain response actually produces a hypoalgesic (pain lessening) effect. Swearing reduced cold-pressor latency by a similar amount in males and females, but led to a greater reduction in perceived pain in females and a greater increase in heart rate in females. However, the most intriguing sex difference was the observation that a hypoalgesic effect of swearing was present in females irrespective of the tendency to catastrophise, whereas in males the hypoalgesic effect of swearing dissipated as the tendency to catastrophise increased. A diminishment in swearing-related hypoalgesia with increased catastrophising may occur because negative emotions induced by swearing spill over into catastrophic thinking in individuals more predisposed towards catastrophising. Nevertheless, it is unclear why the sex difference occurred.

As previously found, male participants generally showed lower levels of catastrophising than females, although the range of catastrophising scores in both the sexes was wide. That men swear more often than women may be pertinent. Fear of pain predicted perceived pain in the nonswearing condition, consistent with previous research. However, fear of pain did not predict perceived pain in the swearing condition. This interesting finding suggests that a part of the hypoalgesic effect of swearing may be because of the amelioration of that part of increased pain perception that is brought about by fear of pain, although further research would be required to investigate this further.

Next we consider the role of emotion in the hypoalgesic effect of swearing. In considering its neurobiological underpinnings Pinker suggests that swearing aloud may tap into 'deep and ancient parts of the emotional brain', particularly the limbic system and the basal ganglia of the right hemisphere. Certainly, swearing often occurs within a strong negative emotional context. The influence of negative affect on pain has been well researched although with inconsistent results: negative emotions produce hypoalgesia in some studies, but the opposite effect of hyperalgesia in others. Rhudy and Meagher suggest that hypoalgesia occurs only if the negative emotion experienced in the context of a painful stimulus is sufficiently strongly felt to cause fear rather than anxiety. For instance, they observed a stress-induced hypoalgesic response to radiant heat pain after feareliciting electric shocks. It was suggested that fear, being an immediate alarm reaction to present threat, leads to a fight or flight response including heart rate acceleration, whereas anxiety,

being a future oriented emotion, is characterized by a less activated state of hypervigilance and somatic tension. Neurobiologically, fear may cause amygdala activation of descending pain inhibitory systems that regulate the flow of incoming nociceptive signals. Therefore, perhaps swearing induces a negative emotion that, if not fear, may nevertheless be characterized as an immediate alarm reaction to present threat. The heart rate acceleration after swearing observed in this study is consistent with activation of the fight or flight response. However, the question as to which negative emotion swearing elicits, if not fear, is unclear. One possibility is aggression. Everyday examples of aggressive swearing include the football manager who 'psychs-up' players with expletive-laden team talks, or the drill sergeant barking orders interspersed with profanities.

Swearing in these contexts may serve to raise levels of aggression, downplaying feebleness in favour of a more pain-tolerant machismo, most likely mediated by classic fight or flight mechanisms. No studies have investigated the effect of manipulating level of aggression on pain tolerance although the reverse has been examined. Electric shock pain tolerance was established in a group of men and the same individuals chose what level of electric shock they would be willing to administer to a fellow participant. The correlation between the highest tolerated and the highest administered shock was $r=0.32$, indicating that higher levels of pain tolerance predicted increased aggression. Future research could usefully examine whether invoked aggression induces hypoalgesia.

"This study has shown that, under certain conditions, swearing produces a hypoalgesic effect.Swearing may have induced a fight or flight response and we speculate on a role for aggression in this. In addition swearing nullified the link between fear of pain and pain perception"

EPILOGUE

You, the reader, have just
completed an expletive filled
tour through the world
of swearing.
Congratu-fucking-lations!
We have covered the beginnings of man, the first curses
of organised religion,
swearing in popular culture
and even those who tried to
ban it. However, you could
say that was the tip of the
fucking iceberg. There's much
more behind a simple, honest
four letter word like "shit".
Swearing is a really important
part of one's life, it would be
impossible to imagine going
through life without swearing
and without enjoying the odd

swear now and then. There is an array of reasons as to why you might swear, be that physical pain or emotional distress, that will benefit from the power of swearing. There's a whole process in your brain happening in that moment and it's happening for a good reason. "That ballbusting castrating son of a cunt bitch made me work late every fucking day this week for not a single penny more!", that, or any similar sentence, could be a line that crossed your mind at some point. Cursing your boss, your colleague, the bus, your wife, your kids, your dog, your car even yourself it's

fine, it's actually a great thing
to do. Do it and you'll see it
does something to and for you.
There's a process in your brain
that'll make you feel better.
Science is still trying to figure
the tiny details of how this
all really works, but who
gives a crap about that. What
they do know for sure is that
swearing reduces pain and
that this pain reduction is
due to our "fight or flight"
response in our brain. The
body's way of saying 'let's get
up and go'. Enough said in
my opinion. Swearing is awesome, it reduces mental and
physical pain, it makes you
feel great, it's stress relieving,

it has been there since man, since language, since forever, it's natural, its instinctive and I think it's pretty fabulous. Funny then, that there still are mad, silly, prissy people who say swearing is a sign of a poor vocabulary. This is such utter bullshit. If anything people who swear the most tend to have the widest vocabulary and the kind of people who maintain the contrary tend to have a pretty poor vocabulary themselves. Human behavioral studies about the usage of swear words in our language also suggest that people who use a lot of swear words actually tend to be more honest and trust worthy.

Same thing with people who claim that it's not necessary to swear. Again, total non-sense. It's not necessary to listen to music, it's not necessary to make art, it's not necessary to have colored socks, but is anyone going to say "I was shocked to see his colored socks, they weren't necessary!". No. Ain't going to happen. Things not being necessary is what makes life interesting. The little extras in life, the small pleasures and exciting forms of expres-sion . They should make us feel pumped about being here.

We should see swearing as a pleasure in life!
What we can conclude is that the sort of tweedy silly person who's backward in development and so still thinks that swearing is in any way a sign of a lack of education or of a lack of verbal interest is just a fucking lunatic. Because it's the fucking reverse, it's a sign for a healthy brain and a highly functional speech centre in one's brain. I think it's a beautiful thing if someone is able to use a variety of swear words and create a nicely sounding, well structured and crushing powerful swearing sentence

"Frankly my dear i don't give a damn". It's almost fucking poetry.

After dealing with the whole swearing topic just for some time I already have to admit that I think something went totally wrong in the past, shit got out hand. Censorship,banning, hilarious fines all that jazz, the way some groups of people, governments and all the institutions of power think about swearing and handle it nowadays is totally the wrong way to do it. In fact, there are many fucking brilliant reasons that show that no doubt, we should start swearing now. People who don't swear should better start immediately doing it and people who already swear, well done, great job, but go and swear some more from now on. The more the merrier. "Without powerful curse words, human beings will again be throwing sticks and stones and trying to break eath other's bones!", Dr. Aman pretty much nailed it with that statement and trust me that son of a bitch knows what he's talking about and he is absolutely fucking right. All of us should adapt all forms of cursing and swearing and incorporate them into our daily life to feel better, happier, to make our world a better place and yourself a better person. Your supposed to feel fucking great already. Start swearing now. Trust me and fuck you very much.

Sincerely yours,
the Author

FUCK YOU VERY MUCH!

Published in 2017 by **B/S** Publishers
a book by Anna-Maria Kiosse

BIS Publishers
Building Het Sieraad
Postjesweg 1
1057 DT Amsterdam
The Netherlands

T: 31 (0)20515 02 30
bis@bispublishers.com
www.bispublishers.com

ISBN: 978-90-6369-467-8

First printing in 2017
Copyright© Anna Maria Kiosse & BIS Publishers

Concept & Design: Anna Maria Kiosse
www.annakiosse.com